To Bill and Nancy,
Hope you enjoy the book!
Mike Waller
9/9/16

Bill & Nancy -
In honor of
faith, love &
support -
Sue Cocoma

Lorraine Walsh Vonmizele

DURAND, ILLINOIS

Triumph
ON
BAKER ROAD

How the Walsh Family
Defeated Polio

By Rose Walsh Landers
and Mike Waller

With Sue Walsh Cocoma

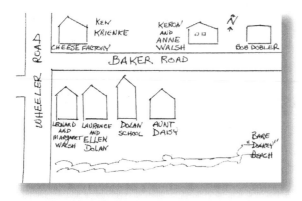

First Edition

ISBN-13: 978-1535408615
ISBN-10: 1535408618

Library of Congress Control Number: 2016941822

Book designed and produced by Jean D. Dodd

Printed in the United States of America
By createspace.com

Contents

Chapter	Title	Page
1:	"I See Snakes"	7
2:	Growing Up	13
3:	Faith and Fun	21
4:	Brown Paper Bag #1	35
5:	The Dreaded Disease	39
6:	Brown Paper Bags #2, #3, #4 and 5	43
7:	"Strike It Rich"	57
8:	Cards, Letters and Visitors	63
9:	Off to Chicago	75
10:	Much to Be Thankful For	85
11:	A Reunion for Dave and Ed	93
12:	A New Crisis	99
13:	A Special Graduation	103
14:	Celebrating Durand's Centennial	111
15:	Broken Hearts	125
16:	Home at Last	131
17:	More Broken Hearts	143
18:	Tom Dolan's Poem	149
19:	How Did We Defeat Polio?	153
20:	Life Resumes	157
21:	Whatever Happened to All of Us?.	163
EPILOGUE: Rose's Story		185
NOTES		203
ACKNOWLEDGEMENTS		219
ABOUT THE AUTHORS		221

Dedication

    This important story from my family's history is dedicated to my three children — Bridget, Matthew and Michael — and five grandchildren —Kieran, Connor, Evelyn, Colin and Nora — so that they may pass it on to their children's children. Let us never forget my parents', Keron and Anne Walsh, strength and reliance on their faith during our polio crisis in 1955-1957. One of your Grandma Anne Walsh's favorite quotes was "It is the set of our sails and not the wind which determines the way we go." Your Grandpa and Grandma Walsh weathered our terrible storm by setting their sails with their strong faith and love for their family. Their dedication to their 14 children lives on in each of you. This extraordinary story about our ordinary farm family is an important thread in our beautiful tapestry. It is an example of perseverance for generations to come.

Rose Walsh Landers
April 1, 2016

CHAPTER 1:

"I See Snakes"

I t was hot.
Blistering hot.
100+-degrees hot.
So hot was it in the summer of 1955 that tar bubbles were bursting nearly every day on blacktopped Baker Road five miles northeast of the town of Durand, Ill., where Keron and Anne Walsh and their 14 children lived on their family farm.

Temperatures reached into the 90s on 32 days in July and August and hit 100, 102 and 103 on three days, unheard of for Northern Illinois.

Our feet stuck to the road as we took our daily walks to visit Aunt Daisy Walsh, one of dad's two sisters. The bottoms of our shoes were black by the time we arrived at her back door, even though her house was only about two football fields up the road from our big white farmhouse. Aunt Daisy's house was so close that we could hear her radio as she listened to the Milwaukee Braves baseball games.

The Braves were hot, too, in 1955, as Hank Aaron and his 40 home runs led them to a second place finish behind the Brooklyn Dodgers in the National League.

The stifling heat made Bare Donkey Beach more popular than ever.

Our oldest brothers, teenagers Dave and Ed, carved out a swimming hole in Otter Creek about a quarter-mile south on the dirt lane from the farmhouse. In the deepest part of the creek, commonly known by most Durand kids as North Creek, they tied a "Tarzan" rope on an overhanging tree so they could swing out and drop into the cool water. They and our first cousins, Tom and Mike Dolan, and their town buddies put up a sign on the creek's bank that read:

Then all of them — Dave and Ed and Tom and Mike, our second cousins Jack Walsh and Bob Haggerty, and Norm Chilton, Bob Diehl and Bill Rogers — vowed they would refer to the creek only as Bare Donkey Beach when around their parents. Years later Tom said they majored in skinny-dipping, camping, singing, jokes and fun at the beach.

The boys also built a rock dam across the creek to make the water deep enough for jumping off a diving board — a plank, really — just below the hanging Tarzan rope for those who weren't brave enough to take the 12-foot plunge from the rope into the water. Shortly after installing the plank, a rare accident occurred. Donnie Miller dove off the board and lost his glasses. Everyone joined in the under-water search, but the mud had sucked them up.

Often the boys camped overnight near the creek. One morning after an overnight outing Ed was up early and milked a cow in the pasture. He collected the milk in a quart jar, twisted on the lid and stuffed it in the creek to cool. The boys used it for their cereal. "It wasn't half-bad," Jack Walsh remembered.

Other than swimming, arm-wrestling was a favorite beach sport. Few ever toppled Ed, who despite being smaller (about 5-foot 7-inches tall but boasting enormous biceps), was strong beyond his size. Even the much huskier Bob Haggerty rarely beat Ed.

Down the creek to the west and around a curve closer to the Walsh farmhouse the water was much shallower under a small wooden bridge that lacked side rails. The banks were gently sloping, not steep like those at Bare Ass Beach, making it easy to walk down to the water. It was a favorite spot for us girls to wade and swim, only a short walk from the farmhouse. All in all, a great spot to cool off in the blistering heat. But not all of Julie Walsh's memories of the creek are fond:

"Mother forbid us little ones from swimming in the creek unless we asked first and an older person was going with us. Well, some of us snuck over to the creek one afternoon. When we got home Mother lined us up in the back room and said she was so disappointed in us. She said she had to spank us so we would understand not to do this again. She felt as bad as we did. She had us put out our open hands and smacked them with a ruler. It was the only 'spanking' I ever got. All of us cried and we never sneaked off to the creek again."

Our sister Alice also had a testy encounter with the creek. Once while sitting on the bank a caterpillar crawled into one of her new back-to-school shoes. She kicked hard to dislodge it but the shoe went flying into the creek. No one ever did find it.

Once in a while, some of us walked farther west of the bridge, along the creek to the area known as rock bottom. The rocky creek bottom was where the Angus cows liked to cross it in this part of the pasture. If we were feeling brave, we waded in and crossed it, too, being careful to keep our balance on the slippery rocks. We always hoped to avoid the danger lurking in the water — blood suckers. As soon as we got home we inspected the soles of our feet. Screams punctured the air when a leech was discovered. The slimy black worm-like things were disgusting as they feasted on our blood. Mom admonished us to "stay away from rock bottom" as she pulled the blood suckers off our feet.

The summer heat continued. Men working in the fields suffered terribly, complaining at night of exhaustion and headaches. Joe Walsh, the son of Uncle Leonard and Aunt Margaret, was stricken by heat stroke while working in the haymow.

Alice and Anne were excited when they got an invitation to escape the heat. Aunt Margaret, Uncle Leonard and their daughter Mary Lou invited them on a week-long trip to northern Michigan.

"We were thrilled," Anne remembered. "It was probably our first vacation. We prepared our suitcases for a week."

But suddenly, tragic news interrupted and their vacation was delayed.

Marian Walsh called our house on July 12 and asked that we come over to their farm. Uncle Jay was lighting a cigarette in the cow yard when he fell over lifeless. The rescue squad could not revive him.

Mom thought Jay's death was almost more than the entire family could bear — so sudden, so beyond help. He was only 63 years old.

Jay, formally named Jerome, was one of Dad's six brothers. For years, Dad and Jay, with brothers George and Leonard, worked as a team on their farms. Jay and Aunt Nita never had any children of their own but helped raise George's children, Marian and Bob Walsh, after George's wife died young.

After the funeral, the next couple of weeks passed quickly, leading to what our older sisters considered a second Christmas — the opening day of school.

They all loved to go back to school in their new clothes. They waited anxiously for rural mail carrier Floyd "Bump" Sarver to pull in the driveway with boxes of new dresses, jeans, underwear and socks purchased from Montgomery Ward's catalogue. They gathered their new school supplies and discussed who their new teachers and classmates would be.

Lorraine, 18, had graduated from Durand High School in May of 1955 as valedictorian, had worked the summer at Alden's Department Store in Rockford and was preparing to attend Edgewood College in

Madison, Wis. Dave, 17, was entering his senior year and Ed, 16, his junior year. Twins Alice and Anne, 14, were sophomores and twins Joan and Julie, 13, were freshman. Sue, 11, was starting 7th grade, Bill, 10, was entering 6th grade and Bernie, 7, was beginning 3rd grade. It was 6-year-old Tom's turn to enter the 1st grade. Rose, 5, Fran, 3 and Molly, almost 2, were still too young to go to school.

No longer did they attend Dolan School, the one-room schoolhouse located on Baker Road about half-way between Aunt Daisy's home and the Dolan farm, in which one teacher taught all classes from first grade to eighth grade. One year the school's only students were Uncle Leonard and Aunt Margaret's four children —Joe, Jim, Jerry and Mary Lou — and their dog, Tippy, who they trained to sit in a desk. Over the years, various teachers boarded next door with Aunt Daisy. But in 1952 the Durand school district closed the last of the 14 one-room schoolhouses in Laona and Durand townships and bused all the rural students to Durand's schools.

The night before the opening day of school, the Dolans dropped by for a short visit. Rose told her cousin Charlotte that she wasn't feeling well. Charlotte stayed away from Rose the rest of the evening for fear of getting sick and missing the first day of school.

The next morning, on Thursday, Sept. 1, the big day arrived. Everyone was scampering around the house getting ready to catch the school bus when five-year-old Rose woke up and announced to Alice:

"I see snakes."

Dad and his 14 children at the Madison, Wis., zoo in the summer of 1954. Front row from left are: Rose, Bernie and Tom. Middle row, from left: Julie, Alice, Joan, Sue, Bill and Anne, holding Fran. Anne, holding Fran. Back row, from left: Lorraine, Dave Ed and Dad, holding Molly. (Walsh family photo).

Fran, left, and Rose in our front yard in 1954. (Walsh family photo).

CHAPTER 2:

Growing Up

"Life is grand when you live in Durand."

That was the mantra of Ward Waller, the other rural carrier in the town of about 600 people who delivered the mail to the area's farm families.

Life indeed was grand, and much simpler than today. In the late 1940s and early 1950s, it was the Age Before Technology. Cable television, cell phones, personal computers, the internet, Facebook, Twitter, air conditioning, indoor plumbing in many homes, seat belts and air bags in cars, video games and bottled water didn't exist. Nor did serious crime, at least not in Durand or on the farm, where no one locked their doors at night.

The cost of living in 1955 seemed manageable. The average income was $4,137 a year, the equivalent of $36,488 in today's dollars. A new house cost $10,950 ($95,903 in today's dollars). A movie ticket was 75 cents, gasoline was 23 cents a gallon and a first-class postage stamp was 3 cents. Milk was 92 cents a gallon, eggs were 27 cents per dozen, a loaf of bread was 18 cents and hamburger on sale sold for 25 cents a pound.

Fast food was in its early stages. Ray Kroc opened his first McDonald's restaurant in July 1955 in Des Plaines, Ill., with a hamburger, French fries and a Coke costing less than 50 cents. Harland "Colonel" Sanders went on the road selling his fried chicken. That very same month Walt Disney opened Disneyland in California. Later that year President Eisenhower increased the minimum wage to $1.00 an hour.

Television was in its infancy. The first television station in Rockford, 19 miles east of Durand, went on the air as WTVO, an NBC affiliate, on May 3, 1953. Two years later the favorite television shows were all on CBS stations: "The $64,000 Question," "I Love Lucy" and "The Ed Sullivan Show." The first television set in Durand was owned by Bob Haggerty's dad, Francis "Ted" Haggerty, who with Jack Walsh's dad, John Walsh, owned the Chevrolet and John Deere dealership in town. Ted won the TV set with a 75-cent raffle ticket at a dealer's meeting in 1949 in Chicago.

Into this age of innocence marched Dave and Ed Walsh and their cousins Tom and Mike Dolan, teen-age farm boys whose idea of fun was shared by their town buddies, Jack Walsh, Bob Haggerty and Norm Chilton.

At the top of their list was cars, the faster the better. Like most farm boys, Dave started driving a tractor, usually the John Deere M, when he turned 12 or 13. So did Ed and the Dolan boys. And all of them were driving the family cars well before they reached the legal age of 16. Jack and Bob also were driving cars before they turned 16 since their fathers, both cousins of Dad, were car dealers.

Dave and Jack loved to race. Their favorite "track" was the four-mile stretch on Center Street Road at the north end of the town to the Wisconsin state line, on which they spent more than a few nights seeing who could get to the state line the fastest, each in their '48 green Chevys. Racing down the two-lane highway sounded dangerous but even as teen-agers they were experienced drivers and were careful to keep their eyes open for the lights of on-coming cars.

Yale Bridge Road was another favorite racetrack until someone living on the road made a visit to the Chevy dealership and ratted on the boys to John Walsh and Ted Haggerty. Jack and Bob were grounded for three weeks with a warning that each time they asked anything about their cars an extra week would be added to the penalty.

Dave loved to drive Dad's '52 Chevy into town from the mile corner south of town. Just before he reached the bridge over the south branch of Otter Creek at the edge of town, he turned off the key and laughed as the engine backfired, popping like a small cannon. Several such trips demanded a new muffler.

Once Jack was at our cousin Jim Slocum's Gulf Oil Station on the east side of the town square when Dad stopped in. His car needed new tires and he couldn't figure out why they had to be replaced so soon. Jack chuckled. He knew why. You couldn't squeal around the town square late at night and on every county road curve without losing some rubber.

When Dave got his driver's license, Dad let him have the car for an evening with the boys. Dave and Ed picked up Tom and Mike and headed to Durand, where Jack, Bob and Norm joined them. The seven of them crammed into the car and headed west on Highway 75 toward Davis. The road had been plowed but was still snow-covered and slippery.

They met a carload of boys from Dakota, a neighboring town, and one of them lost his hat out the window. Ed picked it up and Dave sped off with the Dakota boys in hot pursuit. Dave managed to negotiate a slight curve down the road but the Dakota car wasn't so lucky — it slid into the snow-filled ditch. Dave turned his car around and returned to the crash scene. The Durand boys helped pull the Dakota car out of the snow and gave back the hat. Only the Dakota boys' pride was hurt.

The Durand boys engaged in more than their share of pranks, especially around Halloween. One year they decided Town Square Park in the village needed an outhouse. They had one in mind—the outhouse at Dolan School, the one-room schoolhouse on Baker Road that was now vacant.

Jack "borrowed" his dad's truck and trailer at the Chevy dealership, drove the five miles out to Dolan School and, with Dave, Ed, Tom, Mike and Bob riding shotgun, loaded the outhouse on the trailer.

Instead of driving back to town on Center Street Road, Jack took another route and arrived in Durand just west of St. Mary's Catholic Church on West Main Street. Norm served as the lookout man stationed by the Methodist Church at the north end of the town square. When the coast was clear (no one was in the square and the county police were gone for the night), Norm drove up the hill on Main Street toward St. Mary's and signaled an all-clear to Jack by flashing his car lights. They unloaded the outhouse in the center of Town Square Park, returned the truck and trailer to the dealership across the street and went home.

The next day Mayor Raymond Meissen decided the village square was no place for an outhouse and had it removed to the end of East Washington Street on the outskirts of town. But Tom Spelman, a buddy of Ed's, and some of his friends thought the outhouse was a perfect match for Town Square Park and decided to move it back the next night.

Somehow word got back to the powers-that-be that Tom Spelman and his friends were planning such a caper. So the mayor, a policeman, Mr. Kaiser, and other civic watchdogs kept a vigil with the blinds pulled down in Bill Steward's barbershop on the west side of the square. Just after midnight, Tom and his buddies appeared and began unloading the outhouse. Out of the barbershop rushed the vigilantes, who surrounded and arrested Tom and his gang. They carted them off to the Winnebago County jail in Rockford. Their parents had to bail them out in the middle of the night.

Tom's dad, Leo Spelman, who with Rod Doty owned the Ford dealership and the DX Gas Station, was unhappy with the turn of events. He saw Jack the next morning and blamed Tom's misfortune on him. Leo was sure it was Jack and his buddies who put the outhouse in the park in the first place. Jack denied having any idea what Leo was talking about.

Their pranks weren't confined to Town Square Park. Once, after taking Dave home after a late night out, Jack and Bob accompanied Dave to his bedroom upstairs. They tossed him on the bed and yanked out the long single hair that had been in the middle of his chest for years. Jack and Bob then raced down the stairs, out the door and headed home. Asked years later if alcohol had been involved in the episode, Jack said he didn't remember.

Like the boys in town, Dave and Ed and Tom and Mike attended various events in Durand. On Sunday nights, they often drove to Legion Field to watch the Durand Merchants fast-pitch softball team thrash some outstanding team from Rockford, Beloit or Freeport. Huge crowds, many parked in cars lined up along the left- and right-field foul lines, came to see one of the best teams in Northern Illinois and Southern Wisconsin.

In 1939, long before the Merchants became famous, Dad was their manager. Baseball was his favorite sport and favorite game to play with us. He seemed like Superman when batting balls over the 53-foot high windmill in the driveway. We were all excited when he paused on his way from the barn to the house, set down his milk pail, went to the garage and returned with his bat and ball. We all ran to chase the balls, which sometimes ended up across the road.

On summer evenings, our big front yard was transformed into our own "field of dreams." Dad umpired from the nearby steps with Mom sitting beside him. Home plate was close to them at the northeast corner of the yard. The boys were pitcher and catcher and the girls covered the infield and outfield. The ditch marked the home run line on the south side, the cow lot fence on the west side. Ed was a good hitter. Our cousin Joe Walsh often told Bernie how much he enjoyed watching Ed play baseball, always adding that "Ed was a very good athlete." At the end of the game Dad batted balls to the outfield. We all fielded them; he made sure to hit them to all sides of the yard.

Another sport the boys enjoyed was basketball. They often shot baskets with their friends in the haymow. Ed was a pretty good shot, much better than Dave. Dad insisted they have the opportunity to play on the school teams even though he could use their full-time help on the farm. Both played on the junior high and freshman-sophomore basketball teams but neither was a star, like Norm Chilton.

The boys' favorite activity was hunting, especially for ducks and geese. Dave and Ed each had a 12-gauge double-barrel shotgun. Tom had a 20-gauge shotgun and Mike had a .410 shotgun. Jack Walsh often joined them, proudly packing his handsome .410 three-shot Remington shotgun that was a gift from our Great Uncle Billy Walsh. Dad and Uncle Laurence Dolan spent lots of time teaching the boys how to use the guns properly.

They often would go hunting in the nearby woods for squirrels in the fall and rabbits in the winter. Mike remembered his mom, Aunt Ellen, soaking the squirrels in salt water before frying them. They didn't taste too bad, Mike said.

One evening Norm Chilton was bowling at Durand's four-lane bowling alley when Ed came in, obviously very excited. He had heard ducks and geese down in the bottoms near the farm, he told Norm, and they should hightail it down there before sun-up. That was fine with Norm — he'd be there.

Dave and Ed were ready to go the next morning when Norm arrived. They walked east from the farm to the Dobler farm and arrived at a swampy area, with water up to their knees. A 50-gallon drum with an open top was sticking out of the water in the middle of the swamp. Dave waded out and climbed into the barrel to get closer to the ducks. Norm and Ed stayed on the edge of the swamp. Dave's decision was a good one — within minutes he shot several teal ducks.

Just in time, too, because as he was gathering his bounty they spotted an old truck with a steaming radiator headed toward them.

Dave met the truck at the edge of the swamp. Out of it leaped Bob Dobler and his dad, George, who informed the boys that this was Dobler land and they would have to leave. They did, and learned the basic lesson of seeking permission before hunting on someone else's land.

One weekend, Dave, Ed, Norm and Mike Dolan were hunting along Otter Creek. Suddenly a very large bird jumped out in front of them. With the first shot the bird started falling down but managed to keep going. A second shot brought it down closer to the ground but again it struggled to stay upright. With the last round of shots the bird hit the ground. Upon inspection, the boys were shocked to discover they wouldn't be eating the bird for dinner. They had killed a crane.

Another time, Dave, Ed and Norm went duck hunting east of our big meadow. They were in an open area that had a drainage ditch with standing water. The boys could hear the ducks but could not see them. They got down on their stomachs and started crawling toward the squawking. The ducks heard them coming and startled them when about 30 took to the air honking louder than before.

All three hunters fired away. When the smoke settled, they found only one duck. But whose was it? Dave and Ed each had a 12-gauge double-barrel shotgun that fired pellets. Norm had an over/under weapon that shot bullets and pellets. A quick flick of the wrist would change from one ammo type to another. Upon inspection of the duck, it clearly was Norm's — a bullet was lodged in the bird's head.

Bishop Muldoon, during a visit to St. Mary's Church in 1911, with altar boys Keron Walsh, 9, at right and his cousin Ted Haggerty. (Walsh family photo).

The Walsh family farmhouse. (WREX-TV).

Ed, left, and Dave Walsh, before polio struck. (Walsh family photo).

Anne and Keron Walsh in 1958. (Walsh family photo).

Playing cards on their senior class train trip to Washington, D.C., in May 1956 are, from left, Norm Chilton, Bob Haggerty, Jack Walsh and Tom Dolan (photo source unknown).

Buddies Bob Haggerty, left, and Dave Walsh. (Durand High School yearbook).

CHAPTER 3:

Faith and Fun

The Catholic Church and St. Mary's parish in Durand played an important role in our lives. Father Joseph A. Driscoll recruited Dave, Bob Haggerty, Tom Dolan and Dan Waller shortly after their confirmation to become altar boys. Father chose them and not Jack Walsh because at the time the four were about the same height. Jack was much taller then, but within a few years Dave sprouted up to 6-feet, 2-inches, towering over the other three.

Dave and Ed took their religion seriously. After attending the visitation for Uncle Charlie Carroll in December 1954 in Polo, Ill., they rode back to Durand on snow-covered roads with Joe and Florence Walsh. The snow was drifting badly when they came upon a car in a ditch on Highway 75 just a short distance from the turn to Durand on Highway 70. It was Harry Vale, the boys' ag teacher and FFA (Future Farmers of America) adviser.

Dave and Ed jumped out and pushed Mr. Vale's car back onto the road. Because of the bad weather, the boys stayed all night at Joe and Florence's place, at Wheeler and Baker roads just west of the Dolan farm. Before Dave and Ed went to bed, they knelt side by side on their knees and said their prayers. The image stuck forever in Florence's mind.

Fun and games also prevailed at St. Mary's. One Saturday night Jack, Bob and Dave were at church going to confession. They were standing in line under a single light in front of the confessional at the back of the church, waiting their turn. As time dragged on, the giggling, jostling and loud whispers escalated. Suddenly, at the front altar of the dimly lit church a booming voice rang out: "Boys, quiet down!" They thought God had spoken. It was only Father Driscoll, who obviously wasn't in the confessional. His voice was so loud that St. Mary's didn't need a public address system until he left in 1960.

Father Driscoll, who arrived at St. Mary's in 1933, was a large man, about 6-foot 1 inch tall and weighing about 230 pounds. He played to win on the athletic field as hard as he tried to win souls to the church. He was reported to have once been asked by a bishop to quit playing basketball because his Irish temper got the best of him.

Father Driscoll was a member of the original St. Mary's bowling team, which bowled every Monday night at the Durand Bowl starting in 1944 when Pete Adleman built it. Dad, Ward Waller, Ed Hagerty and Maurice Murphy were the other original team members.

"We may not have been the best team but we played the hardest and had the most fun of them all," recalled Waller. "There also was a team from Irish Grove (St. Patrick's Catholic Church, where Father also was pastor) but Father usually bowled with us."

Father's bowling style was anything but traditional. Rather than letting the bowling ball smoothly glide out of his hand on to the alley, he often heaved it hard and bounced it onto the surface. It sounded like a clap of thunder.

The team, often accompanied by Father Driscoll, made several trips over the years to Chicago, 90 miles southeast of Durand, to see the Chicago Cubs play baseball, one of Father's favorite sports. Father also attended Cubs games with Bill Steward, the town barber. "We'd have great talks...he loved to talk," Bill said.

In the summer of 1947, Father Driscoll and five other men — Dad, Dick Highland, Ted Haggerty, Ward Waller and Gerald "Grub" McKearn — attended a Cubs game at Wrigley Field. While driving home, a severe storm hit Durand. Their five wives, each of whom was expecting a baby in the fall, were glad the men made it home safely.

As much as Father enjoyed bowling, he loved even more being umpire at St. Mary's two-week summer school where the parish children studied the Baltimore Catechism. Nuns from Chicago, including Father Driscoll's sister, Sister Mary Eucharista, conducted the classes in the church basement. Each day they sent the four altar boys to the outside well to fetch water in large coffee pots so all the children could have a drink. Bob Haggerty, the king of fun and mischief, pumped the water as slow as possible, making sure it took 30 minutes or more to complete the 10-minute task. Anything, Bob said, to avoid classwork.

Everyone looked forward to recess, when Father stood behind the pitcher and umpired the daily softball game on the vacant lot on the west side of the rectory. His booming voice left little doubt if the pitch was a strike or a ball. If a batter hit the ball into the garden in right field, a double was awarded. No outfielder was allowed to chase down a ball in the garden.

Each day the players waited for someone to hit a ball far enough in left field to break a window in the rectory. One day it finally happened. Bill Flynn smashed a pitch over the heads of all the left fielders (everyone played so sometimes there were eight or nine outfielders) and demolished a window. Everybody told Father they were sure sorry about that, but secretly were delighted.

As the summer wound down, the Trask Bridge picnic and Winnebago County 4-H fair commanded all of our attention.

Every August Dad took all of us to the annual Trask Bridge Picnic, billed as the world's largest country picnic. It was a special treat sponsored by the Burritt Grange and drew folks from all over the region, some years as many as 75,000. Located on farmland adjacent to the Pecatonica River about five miles southwest of Durand, the picnic that began in 1910 had something for everyone: softball and baseball games, a carnival, poultry and baking goods exhibits and games galore. Among them were contests for bundle tying, log chopping, fly casting, hog calling and husband calling.

But the highlight of every summer was the Winnebago County 4-H Fair on the west edge of Rockford. Dave and Ed and the Dolan boys were always active in 4-H clubs and the school FFA chapter. They were members of the Otter Creek Beef Boys 4-H club, founded by Dad when Dave was about 10 and old enough to start showing their Angus beef cattle and Hampshire hogs at the Winnebago County 4-H Fair. Mike and Tom raised and showed Shorthorn cattle.

During monthly 4-H club meetings, members gave demonstrations on various subjects the boys would need to know when they reached the fair, such as how to make a rope halter for a steer and how to groom the animal for showing. The goal was to win a ribbon, the best being the Grand Champion or Reserve Grand Champion. If that was unattainable, a blue, red or white ribbon would be welcomed.

Preparation for the fair started months earlier, when Dave and Ed chose steers from Dad's herd that displayed the most promise of being trained for the show ring and becoming the fair's Grand Champion. When the time came for training the animals to be led by a halter, they were separated from the herd and kept in their own pens in the barn.

Even before showing many animals at the fair, Dave and Ed gained some experience at training them. In the late 1940s, Dad bought a pony for us. She was gentle and we named her Sandy because of her color. Much to our surprise, Sandy was pregnant and delivered a frisky colt we named Sparky. We were so excited when we first saw that little pony with his long spindly legs standing next to Sandy. Sparky was well named because he was a bit on the wild side until Dave and Ed trained him to allow us to climb aboard for a ride. Our brothers seemed to enjoy every minute of the first wild rides on Sparky around the farmyard. On one of Dave's early rides, Sparky was running at full speed through the orchard, with Dave bent fully forward, arms around Sparky's neck, successfully ducking under tree limbs while managing to stay on for a most exciting adventure. After Sparky was trained, we had years of fun with the two ponies, riding through the woods or having them hitched to a buggy or even to a toboggan in winter.

"Steer on the loose!" were the words we did not want to hear in June and July, when Dave and Ed were training their steers. Some steers were easy to tame. Others were just plain ornery. Those were the ones we remember bolting from our brothers and running helter-skelter across the driveway, around the yard and even across the road and down the lane toward the creek. The tractor was often needed to lead the runaway steer home and back in his pen. The rope halter was firmly tied to the back of the tractor, which was driven ever so slowly back to the barn. Once the animals were finally tamed, we helped Dave and Ed shampoo and brush the steers' coats and tails.

When the fair opened, the boys took their animals to the fairgrounds on West State Street. They stayed overnight with their steers, sleeping on the straw next to them, awaiting the next day's events. The crowds in the bleachers surrounding the show rings always made for exciting moments. Sometimes during the fair a steer would break loose and run wildly through the fairgrounds, scaring people until being captured.

Showmanship ability was essential to winning ribbons at the 4-H fair, and Dave excelled at it. He had a very relaxed manner, especially when showing his pigs.

Dave's approach was to bring the pigs into the show area and casually walk over to the fence surrounding the ring. He let the pigs run around, doing whatever they pleased, including pestering the pigs of other contestants. Soon Dave's pigs wore themselves out. Using a gate in one hand and a brush in the other, he moved the pigs into the proper position, brushed the sawdust off them to make them presentable and waited for the judge. The judge was impressed. He especially liked the calm manner of Dave's pigs and awarded him the top Showmanship Prize.

It was so typical of Dave's personality and style. He was laid back but hard-working. Dave always assumed he would be a farmer and help Dad operate our farm. He loved a good time but never caused trouble.

Dave and Ed were very popular leaders at school. In 1953 Dave was elected president of the sophomore class and Ed was elected vice president of the freshman class. In the spring of 1955, when the various clubs held elections for the next school year, both were elected to the student council. Dave was elected president of the FFA chapter, and Ed the treasurer. They were always respectful of their elders, often addressing teachers as "sir."

Ed was much more reserved and studious than Dave. Dad loved playing a "Trivia-like" game with Ed, asking him questions about various subjects. He always tried to stump Ed but seldom could. Classmates enjoyed having Ed sit next to them in Study Hall because he helped them with their algebra. Another reason was that he was so much fun to be around. He and Dave McCullough were friendly rivals in the race to become the class valedictorian. They both took all the hardest classes together and were neck-and-neck when they started their junior year in September 1955.

Arm wrestling wasn't the only activity in which Ed displayed his physical strength. Once when Bill, Bernie and Tom were playing outside, Bill started teasing his little brothers. Ed happened to be nearby and heard Bernie and Tom getting more and more frustrated. Ed intervened by firmly picking up Bill by the collar of his shirt, bringing him face to face and sternly telling him to "cut it out." It was suddenly very quiet with no more teasing.

Ed never mentioned any plans for the future. Some thought he would go to college, maybe become a scientist. Mom thought Ed could possibly attend Notre Dame.

Maybe Ed would be a carpenter; he loved to build things. For a FFA project he built and painted a doghouse for our collie Boots. With Dave's help, he also built their 4-H box. Each summer the box was packed with the essentials for showing their animals at the fair. And Ed made a large lighted shadow box we used during Christmas. For the front of the shadow box he used an ornate gold picture frame and made a manger to fit the scene within the shadow box for our nativity set.

Ed's humor often caught people off guard because he was so quiet. As part of FFA classes, Mr. Vale and Ed judged hogs one day at our farm. They finished and began driving up the hill on Baker Road, which was slippery. Mr. Vale was having trouble moving up the hill when he was startled by Ed's voice in the back seat: "Peel it, sir!" Harry got a kick out of the "sir" part of the request.

Mr. Vale occasionally stayed for lunch when he visited to inspect Dave or Ed's FFA project. He marveled at the size of the kitchen table; he couldn't believe how long it was. It was 8- or 9-feet long and easily seated all 16 of us with stools on the corners for the littlest ones.

4-H was also an important summertime activity for our older sisters, also known as the "big girls." Our long kitchen table would often be covered with their batches of cookies. Each made many test batches before the fair. Anne made mountains of peanut butter cookies. "They were stacked to the ceiling on the refrigerator in an attempt to get three perfectly formed cookies," Anne said. The girls chose the three best cookies from their batches, put them on a plate, covered them with plastic wrap and took them to the fair. They were displayed in the food tents, which the girls checked periodically to discover what ribbons they had won.

Their sewing projects also took a lot of time. They practiced modeling their dresses, skirts, scarves and other clothing at meetings of the Laona Lively Lassies, where they had fun watching other club members model their clothing. Although she had graduated from high school, Lorraine stayed active in 4-H and made a beautiful charcoal gray wool suit. She won a blue ribbon for it and was selected to show it at the State Fair. But since she won a trip to the State Fair a year earlier for her sewing project, she declined to attend the 1955 fair and instead continued working at Alden's.

Our 4-H leaders helped us girls learn many new things but Mom was our first and most important teacher. She was a trained teacher, but a natural teacher to her core. One of her most important lessons was to never give up. She always knew what to try next, when our 4-H baking experiments flopped, and we were in tears. She would patiently help us figure out how to fix a mistake in our sewing projects, sometimes on the way to the fair!

She was so clever that she came up with solutions to problems in the kitchen that would have meant disaster for most. Once when her company was due to arrive soon, she dropped her only jar of Miracle Whip salad dressing, which she was about to use for her potato salad. "No problem," she said as she calmly cleaned up the broken jar and ruined dressing. "I will just make my own mayonnaise," and she did without using a recipe.

Mom also made sure that her girls learned the basics about music, which was very important to her. She had played the clarinet in the orchestra and sang in the Glee Club at St. Joseph's Academy in Guthrie, Okla., where she completed the two-year teacher training course. She relaxed by playing the piano. Her favorite song was Star of the East, which she played each Christmas. She hired Miss Olive Crowley to give piano lessons to our "big girls." They were instructed in our home, on our piano in the living room. Miss Crowley taught each set of twins at the same time. She sat between her two pupils on the piano bench, turning to each one when it was her turn to play. The younger girls took lessons from Mary Louise Green in her home.

A few of us played in the school band instead of taking piano lessons. Some did both band and piano. Mom was delighted when

Ed showed interest in music as well as sports. He learned to play the accordion, as Lorraine did, by taking lessons in Rockford. Ed also sang in the high school chorus.

It was also clear to us that Mom valued education and loved books. In her precious few spare moments, she somehow managed to read. During her busiest years, she preferred the shorter stories in the Reader's Digest condensed books. One of her favorite books was "Mrs. Mike," by the Freedmans. She often told stories from that book, about pioneer life in Alaska. She occasionally read poems to us, from her "My American Heritage," a collection of poems, songs and sayings. "Snowbound" and "Casey at the Bat" were two of her favorites.

Mom was too busy in the house to ever help with farm work. Summer was her harvest season, when her already busy kitchen became a food preservation factory. Dad took care of the vegetable garden and Mom took care of canning and freezing their plentiful produce. By fall the basement shelves were well stocked with her jars of canned tomatoes, green beans, applesauce, two or three varieties of pickles, pears, chili sauce, jams and jellies. The freezer was full of frozen sweet corn, green peas, peaches and strawberries, as well as our own beef and pork. Somehow she still found time to tend to her flower garden. Delphiniums and phlox were her favorites.

One summer for the fair, in addition to sewing and baking, Julie followed Mom's lead and took up flower arranging along with her best friend, Jean Rafferty. But our flowers weren't cooperating at fair time so she didn't have enough for an arrangement. She called Jean, who solved the problem. The girls visited Jean's grandmother's garden at her home in Rockford, where Julie picked a beautiful vase-full of tiger lilies. Off to the fair they went, where Julie won the top prize—a trip to the Illinois State Fair.

"I was so scared and shy that I told Jean she should go because the flowers came from her grandmother's garden," Julie said. "But Jean insisted I go. Dad drove me to the bus station in Rockford where I

joined other State Fair winners on the trip to Springfield. We slept in
fair buildings and I gave my demonstration again. I ended up having a
lot of fun but I was so glad to get home."

But home on Sept. 1, 1955 was about to become scary.

Ed with his 4-H steer. (Walsh family
photo).

Ed, left, and Dave in our barn with their 4-H pigs.
(Walsh family photo).

Dave with his 4-H steer. (Walsh family photo).

30

Dad, left, with all his sons in May 1955, from left: Dave, Ed, Bill, Bernie and Tom. (Walsh family photo).

Ed playing his accordion. (Walsh family photo).

Durand High School in 1955. (DHS yearbook).

FFA (Future Farmers of America) officers in 1954, from left (Tom Dolan, Carlyle Horstmeier, Dave Walsh, teacher Harry Vale, Wayburn Kelsey, Ed Walsh and Phil Kelsey. (DHS yearbook).

DHS Student Council, 1954-55, from left, sitting: Mary Dolan, Lorraine Walsh, Jim Schmerse, Supt. Paul G. Norsworthy and Wayburn Kelsey. Standing from left: Sally Kelsey, Mike Dolan, Jane Walsh, Eunice Wallace, Don Waller, Millie Barker, Joy Hazard, Dave Walsh, Kay Guehring, Bill Haggerty, Roger Sarver and Ron Adleman. (DHS yearbook).

St. Mary Catholic Church, with the rectory at far right. (Photo courtesy of Mo Ostergard and Dennis Bliss).

Durand's Junior High School's heavyweight basketball team in 1952-1953, in front from left: Ed Walsh, Tom Ditzler and Bob Cowan. Standing, from left: Donnie Keller, Jim Waller, Harvey Ostergard, Phil Kelsey and Dick Welch. (DHS yearbook).

33

Durand's Junior High School heavyweight basketball team in 1951-1952, in front from left: Dan Waller, Dave Walsh, Carlyle Horstmeier, Donnie Keller and Dick Welch. Standing, from left: Don Waller, Bob Diehl, Jim Waller, Harvey Ostergard, Phil Kelsey and Bob Peters. (DHS yearbook).

CHAPTER 4:

Brown Paper Bag #1

Mom rushed about collecting all the laundry as the older kids got ready for school on Thursday, Sept. 1. It was wash day, one of her busiest days of the week. She gathered and sorted the many piles of laundry, got the wringer washer and big rinse tub ready and lined up the wooden clothes baskets and wooden clothes pins she used to hang the wash on the clothes lines out the back door. The sun was shining, forecasting a good day to hang the laundry.

Rose started complaining of a terrible headache. Sue was in the living room, waiting for the bus, when Mom asked her to help Rose tie her shoes. Rose was wearing a cute gray and blue plaid dress with a tie belt and a Peter Pan collar. She sat in a large chair in the corner of the living room across from the big green couch. Sue knelt down and tied her shoes.

The bus, driven as usual by Burdette Hanford, pulled into our gravel driveway. One by one everyone except Lorraine and the three little girls scampered on. Lorraine had already started packing her new Samsonite luggage, her high school graduation gift, as she prepared to go to college. Dave and Ed, who had been the first ones up, two hours before the bus arrived, were last ones on. They had finished the morning chores, tossing heavy bales of hay from the haymow in the barn to the cattle and mixing ground oats with water for the pigs. They gobbled down a fried egg sandwich and rushed up the steep narrow stairs to change into their new Montgomery Ward's clothes.

Their teen-aged sisters had been up early, too, sharing the one-upstairs bathroom getting ready for school. Joan and Julie were starting their freshman year and were worried that Rose seemed to have more than just the flu.

Shortly after the bus left, Mom raced to the barn to tell Dad about Rose. She then called Dr. Charles A. Leonard, our family physician for several years. They then changed their clothes, gathered up Rose, 3-year-old Fran and 1 3/4-year-old Molly and drove to Dr. Leonard's office in Rockford.

Dr. Leonard said Rose was very ill and ordered a spinal tap for her at St. Anthony's Hospital. They drove to St. Anthony's and waited for the results of the lab tests. Soon Dr. Leonard appeared in the hall and announced: "Rose is in the first stages of polio. The next 24 hours will be very critical. Take her to Township Hospital, where she will be put into isolation."

Mom remembered asking: "But what about the other children? What can we do?"

"We don't even know how polio is spread," Dr. Leonard replied. "There is nothing we can do. Just wait and see. There is no quarantine. The children should just go to school as usual."

Dad and Mom took Rose to Rockford Township Hospital where they handed her over to a nurse who told them where to wait. After a while the nurse returned with a brown paper bag containing Rose's clothes. She told Dad and Mom they could not visit Rose in her room. The only way to see her was to go outside and step up on a platform under her window where they could see Rose in bed and could talk to her through a screen when the window was open.

Rose was scheduled to stay in isolation for seven days. Mom and Dad stayed for a short time, then bid Rose farewell and drove home in a daze. On the way home, one of the girls, Fran or Molly, reached on the dashboard of the car and grabbed some gum Rose had taken out of her mouth before she went into the doctor's office. The little girl put the gum in her mouth before Mom could stop her. Not for long, though. Mom retrieved it quickly.

Mom didn't wait long to call her youngest sister, Aunt Pat Kenucane in Beloit. "We have just taken Rose to the hospital," Mom said. "She has polio." A few minutes later she ended the conversation by saying, "Well, if none of the other children get it we'll be OK."

Lorraine found out at Highland and Bentley's grocery store in Durand that Rose had contracted polio. Lorraine was dropped off from her car pool after working at Alden's and was waiting for a ride home when Ramona Bentley approached her and said, "I hear your sister Rose has polio."

Dave was helping fill the silo adjacent to the barn, stomping on silage with his cousin Jim Walsh. When he found out Rose had polio, he told Jim, "I hope I never get that."

When Anne, Alice, Joan, Julie and Sue got home from school, they jumped off the bus and rushed into the house to find out about Rose. Mom was standing by the kitchen stove, crying and holding Molly in one arm while washing the top of the stove with her other hand.

"Through her sobs she told us that Rose had polio," Julie said. "All of us started crying because Rose was very sick and could not have visitors, not even her parents. It was so hard for us to imagine and absolutely heart-breaking to think of our little sister so far from home and away from everyone she knew. We were worried someone else in the family would get it too, so all of us pitched in and helped mother with cleaning in an attempt to wash away any polio germs that might be in the house."

It was very quiet in our home that night. We were saying the rosary and trying to keep ahead of the phone calls coming in from people wondering what was going on. The word was spreading fast that Rose had polio. Everybody at school knew by the end of the next day.

For the next several days, Mom and Dad went back and forth to the hospital, climbing the steps outside Rose's room to talk to her. Rose complained of the shots the nurses gave her and wanted to come home. Lorraine stayed at home and took care of the smaller children. She got a big assist from Aunt Daisy, who walked down Baker Road every day to help with the little ones.

During the acute viral phase of polio, nurses at Township Hospital checked Rose's vital signs every day, including monitoring of her temperature, respiratory status, oxygen levels (watching for any need of an iron lung), muscle strength and hydration. Full-time bed rest was the order of the day.

CHAPTER 5:

The Dreaded Disease

You could get polio by swimming in the creek, any creek. Or by swimming in a municipal pool. Or by swimming in any body of water. Or by sitting in the back seat of a moving car next to an open window.

Or by eating unwashed peaches from the grocery story.

This was the conventional wisdom of most parents in 1955, who warned their children of practices that might cause polio.

In truth, few doctors knew then what caused polio. We now know that poliomyelitis, once called infantile paralysis, is a highly infectious disease caused by a virus. It is spread person-to-person by contact with infected secretions from the nose or mouth or with infected feces. It usually enters the body when a person ingests contaminated food or water, or touches the mouth with contaminated hands.

Polio mainly attacks children age five and under. About 90 per cent of patients have only mild symptoms, such as a sore throat, headache, malaise, intestinal upset and fever, and recover completely. In about 1 per cent of cases, the virus attacks nerves inside the spine that send messages to muscles in legs, arms and elsewhere. Spinal polio can result in partial or complete paralysis. If the virus gets into the brainstem, it causes bulbar polio, paralyzing muscles needed for breathing, swallowing and other vital functions. Death may be the result.

No drugs can cure polio once a person is infected. Patients are made as comfortable as possible with bed rest, pain-relieving medications and hot packs to ease the pain of extreme muscle tightness. Some need assistance with breathing, such as supplemental oxygen or a ventilator. In the 1950s, patients with severe breathing problems were placed in an "iron lung," a cylindrical chamber that surrounded the body from the neck down that used rhythmic alterations in air pressure to force air in and out of the lungs.

Rocking beds also helped patients breathe and were not as confining as an iron lung. Using a rocking bed was like riding on a seesaw. The principle was simple: When a patient's head was up and his feet down, the internal organs and diaphragm were pulled by gravity, sucking air into the lungs. When the position was reversed, air was forced out of the lungs.

Polio is best prevented by vaccination. The Salk vaccine, developed by Dr. Jonah Salk at the University of Pittsburgh, was the first to be approved, in 1955. It is made from completely inactive polio viruses and injected into the body.

Dr. Albert Sabin, distinguished service professor at the University of Cincinnati College of Medicine and fellow at the Cincinnati Children's Hospital Research Foundation, developed an oral vaccine made from live but weakened polio viruses. It was introduced in 1962. Both vaccines cause the body to produce antibodies that fight the polio virus.

A third virologist actually developed an oral polio vaccine before Dr. Salk or Dr. Sabin. Dr. Hilary Koprowski, one of the world's foremost biomedical researchers who spent more than 30 years as director of the Wistar Institute in Philadelphia, created a live-virus vaccine that he tested in 1950 on 20 children. Their school for mentally disabled children in Rockland County, N. Y., fearing an outbreak of polio, invited him to vaccinate the children. At the time, approval from the federal government was required to market drugs but not to test them. All went smoothly and none of the children developed polio.

Dr. Koprowski's vaccine was then given to thousands of patients in Africa and Europe with good results. But it never was approved for use in the United States. The reasons? Politics in the medical research world and personality — Dr. Koprowski was a polarizing figure with few advocates in the scientific world.

In addition, Dr. Salk had a huge ally in the race to develop the first approved vaccine. He was backed by funding from the March of Dimes Foundation. It originally was called the National Foundation for Infantile Paralysis and was founded in 1938 by President Franklin D. Roosevelt, who contracted polio in 1921 and remained permanently paralyzed from the waist down for the rest of his life. The foundation's funds and marketing power — it enlisted "poster children" with the disease and celebrities such as Mickey Rooney and Mickey Mouse — gave Dr. Salk the edge he needed.

Within a few years after the Salk and Sabin vaccines, polio all but disappeared in the United States. Pakistan and Afghanistan now stand as the main barrier to global elimination. Outbreaks in 2014 in Syria, Iraq and parts of Africa have been contained, leaving the rest of the world with 54 cases in September 2015. The world never has been closer to eliminating polio.

But polio was thriving in 1955 and was setting up another ambush on Baker Road.

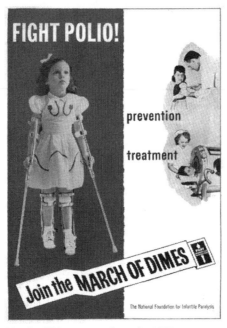

March of Dimes poster from the 1950s.

Advertisement from The Beatrice Daily Sun
(Beatrice, Neb.), Jan. 16, 1951.

CHAPTER 6:

Brown Paper Bags
#2, #3, #4 and #5

About a week after Rose was admitted to Township Hospital, Dave complained one evening that he felt something tingling in his back. He asked Mom if she could see anything.

She saw nothing.

He went upstairs to the bedroom he shared with Ed and was soon asleep in their double bed. The next morning Alice recalled Dave saying his back hurt as he walked down the steep stairway on his way to do chores. He also had a sore throat, headache and stiff neck. It was Friday, Sept. 9.

After all the children except Dave left for school, Mom called Dr. Leonard, who told her to bring Dave to his office on East State Street in Rockford. Dave was so sick that he could barely hold up his head during the drive.

After arriving at Dr. Leonard's office, the doctor examined Dave, asking him to lower his head until his chin touched his chest.

He could not do it.

A spinal tap was needed immediately. The doctor sent them to St. Anthony's. The painful spinal tap confirmed that "Dave, our 6-foot, 2 ½-inch, 17-year-old son, beginning his senior year at Durand High School, had polio," Mom wrote.

Dr. Leonard sent them to Township Hospital, a 20-minute ride down State Street to just outside Rockford's north city limits. Upon arrival a nurse met Dave and escorted him away.

"We again waited until she returned and handed us a brown paper bag containing Dave's clothes" Mom said.

This brown bag, with Dave's size 10 shoes in it, was much heavier than Rose's bag had been. Mom handed it to Dad.

The nurse said Dave was put in the same room with Rose and repeated the rule: no visitors in the room. They could see both of them by going to the same outside window they had been using to "visit" Rose.

They hurried outside to the window and "looked at our two children who a few days ago seemed healthy and happy," Mom said. "We knelt on the crude wooden steps and prayed to God to help our stricken children."

That morning when Dave's high school chemistry teacher, Glenn Slabaugh, realized he was absent he asked Ed where his brother was. "He's at home with a sore throat," Ed said. "Oh, no," replied a startled Mr. Slabaugh.

By the end of the day nearly everyone at school knew Dave was in the hospital with polio. Folks in Durand at the grocery stores, the post office, the barber shop and the gas stations talked about little except that Dave Walsh had also been stricken with polio.

Fear showed up at school like a creeping fog. Many of the guys thought about all the things they did with Dave, especially swimming at Bare Ass Beach, and were scared they might get polio, too. Almost immediately the boys stopped playing touch football.

Fear also kept many people from going into our house, but did not deter the tight-knit group of Dad and Mom's closest family members. Over the past week, they had already closed ranks to encircle them with love and support. With the news of Dave's hospitalization, the circle grew tighter and the safety net of support grew stronger.

Dad's nephews, Joe and Bob Walsh, had already started to help him do the chores so he would have more time for trips to Rockford.

Soon after hearing the latest news, Aunt Margaret knocked at the door. She had brought clean sheets for all our beds and started changing all of them. She even put a sheet on the living room couch, in case one of us might start to feel sick.

Aunt Teresa Houghton, Mom's sister and a registered nurse, came to our house one morning, wanting to help. However, Uncle Bill and she now had a family of their own to consider. They had just adopted their son Jimmy and didn't want to take any chances that he might come down with polio. So she stood outside and talked to Mom through the porch window.

On Saturday, Sept. 10, when Mom and Dad went to visit Dave and Rose at Township Hospital, they were told that Rose was now ready to be transferred to the pediatric unit at St. Anthony's Hospital. She had improved enough to start having more physical therapy.

When the nurse handed Rose to Mom, she was stunned.

"I was shocked to feel her in my arms — limp, like a rag doll," Mom said.

They drove Rose to St. Anthony's and handed her over to the supervisor of pediatrics, Sister Grace, and pediatric nurses who were ready with a stretcher to take her to her room. They transferred her to her bed and immediately placed sandbags along her legs and back.

Mom asked Sister Grace, "How is Rose?"

"That depends on what you mean by how is she," replied the nun, never answering the question. This cold response was typical of Sister Grace's military-style of managing her pediatric unit. She demanded strict adherence to her rigid visiting hours.

After saying goodbye to Rose, Mom and Dad returned home. Ed had been squirrel hunting and he bagged one "over south." He asked Mom to cook it the next day. When Ed got up the next morning, he complained of feeling very tight across his chest.

It was nearly noon Sunday when Mom and Dad returned to

Rockford to visit Rose at St. Anthony's. They planned to visit Dave at Township on their way home. After seeing Rose, Mom phoned Dr. Leonard to inquire about Dave.

"He's in a critical stage," the doctor said. "I would prefer he have no company."

Then Mom mentioned Ed's sore chest.

"Do not go to Township Hospital to see David," the doctor replied, "but go straight home and bring Ed in for a spinal tap at St. Anthony's."

Mom and Dad did as they were told, barely stopping to say goodbye to Rose, who was very quiet, her eyes larger than usual.

"Our whole mind and body wanted to see David," Mom said. "But instead we drove home, put Ed in the car and took him to St. Anthony's."

A spinal tap was performed, and Mom and Dad waited again for the results. Dr. Leonard came down the hall with the bad news: Ed had an even more severe case of polio than either Dave or Rose.

As instructed, Mom and Dad drove to Township Hospital "for the third time in eight days to deliver our second oldest son, age 16, a brilliant boy with sterling qualities, a boy who would never again go hunting or taste a meal of squirrel," Mom said.

Mom and Dad again waited. A nurse soon arrived and presented them with another brown paper bag, this one holding Ed's clothes.

They were told to go to a different set of steps outside the hospital where they could look through the open window to talk to Ed. After visiting awhile, they went to the steps outside Dave's window to visit with him. He had been in the hospital only a day but already some of his friends had visited at the window, unaware of the doctor's orders.

After a short visit with Dave, Mom and Dad "hurried home to tell Father Driscoll that we wished him to say a mass for the children," Mom said. "I told him then that I didn't think I could stand it if we had to take Dave out of the hospital in the condition Rose was in."

Father Driscoll acted immediately. He scheduled a triduum, a series of special religious observances in the Catholic Church over the next three days starting on Monday.

Life at home began rapidly changing as Monday arrived. Dr. Leonard ordered a quarantine for all the children at home and a close watch on those suspected of already having at least mild cases of polio — Anne, twins Joan and Julie, Sue, Frances and Molly.

The quarantine disappointed first-grader Tom.

"I was (at school) three days and then I had to quit," he said.

Despite the quarantine, many friends and neighbors flocked to our house, bringing food and money. A few people who were helping with the chores decided to stay away, forcing Anne and Bill to take on some of the work of feeding the animals and milking the cows.

Lorraine, with help from Aunt Daisy, was taking care of our brothers and sisters at home. She gave up on her plan of attending Edgewood College. A few weeks later the college refunded all her money.

Monday morning was barely unfolding when a phone call came from Dr. Leonard, urging Mom and Dad to return to the hospital.

Dave was burning up with a fever and needed immediate surgery.

Mom and Dad rushed to Township Hospital, where they signed papers authorizing a tracheotomy for Dave.

They were not allowed to see Dave or Ed but from the hall they could watch the activity — Dr. Glenn Smith, a surgeon from St. Anthony's, entering the isolation ward where Dave had been moved, bottles of blood being wheeled in and nurses scurrying everywhere. Dr. Leonard was standing by. A priest from Rockford's St. Peter's Catholic Church, Father Phillip O'Neill, entered the ward and anointed Dave with the last rites.

"Soon the familiar figure of Father Driscoll appeared and he spoke as he hurried into the isolation ward," Mom said. "Next a strange looking machine was hauled into the room, a machine that we were to become very familiar with—the iron lung, a cylindrical-shaped thing with little glass windows across the top and a hole at the end. The machine could be opened the length of one's body.

"We were told later that Dave was placed in the iron lung because he could not breathe on his own and the machine would do it for him. The tracheotomy provided a hole in his throat into which a tube was inserted and a nurse stood by to suction out the fluid that kept accumulating, preventing Dave from breathing.

"He was drowning in his own fluids.

"Dave's body was enclosed in the iron lung and his head was pushed out the open end. He was completely paralyzed and unable to swallow. When the doctors and priests came out, we were told nothing short of a miracle would get Dave back on his feet," Mom said.

Dave was in an oxygen tent as well as an iron lung and polio had paralyzed his lungs. At one point, Dr. Leonard said, Dave turned blue for over 30 seconds. Even if he recovered, he could wind up with permanent brain damage.

The good news was that the tracheotomy and use of the suction machine were effective treatments. Dave was able to breathe better and was stabilized for now.

Meanwhile, the national press had begun reporting on our family's ordeal. Stories by the Associated Press and United Press started appearing in newspapers all over the country.

"We have to keep quiet around the house now," seven-year-old Bernie told reporter Bill Barnum of *The Beloit Daily News*. "We have to stay out of trouble, too. Our house was noisy before all this happened. But now it's awful quiet."

Explaining how he and his six-year-old brother Tom helped out at home, Bernie told *The Daily News* that some of his sick sisters "stayed in bed most of the time…sometimes we carry their meals up on trays."

Tom added: "A neighbor just sent over a tiddlywinks set."

Speaking to a *Chicago Herald-American* reporter, Dad said: "I can't understand it. My children are the only children in the hospital with polio. It's as though we were picked out."

The county Public Health Department couldn't understand it, either. It checked our home, our water supply and our septic system frequently during the first days of the outbreak but never could identify a source for the disease.

Meanwhile, Dr. Leonard was working around the clock. Handling a family with several cases of polio was not new to him. Ten years earlier his own family — 10 children — was struck by the disease. His namesake, Charles Jr., died and five of his other children had been in serious condition. All had bulbar polio, the most serious kind, the same kind that attacked both Dave and Ed.

The doctor checked not only on all of us in the hospital but also on everyone back on the farm. He downplayed his role in the press. "I'm only a family doctor, a clinician who can only hope to guide these children through the acute phase of polio and attempt to escape or minimize the crippling consequences," he told reporters.

He praised the nurses in the isolation ward, the only one of its kind in Winnebago County. All of them had special training or experience treating polio patients and some had answered a televised appeal by the hospital's superintendent for more nurses to meet the emergency situation.

"Those nurses are very good," Dr. Leonard said. "They're giving much more than their share."

Dr. Leonard told reporters it would be useless to give any of us the Salk vaccine now because it would take too long to become effective.

At least Bernie had been vaccinated. In April Bernie and all the first- and second-grade students in Winnebago County schools were bused to West Rockford High School to be vaccinated. The vaccine was in such short supply in 1955 that it had to be rationed.

"There were hundreds of kids our age (about 6 or 7 years old) lined up in single-file lines on the front lawn of West High School," Bernie recalled. "We went through the lines, (received the injections), got back on the bus and went back to Durand." Each of them was given a bright new 1955 penny.

When the school doors in Durand opened on Tuesday morning, Sept. 13, students discovered a notice had been posted in all the classrooms. It read:

> "There will be a special Rosary for the Keron Walsh family in St. Mary's Catholic Church in Durand this evening at 8:00 O'clock P.M. Central Daylight Time.
> "There will be a special Prayer Service this evening at 7:30 P.M. in the Durand Methodist Church, for the Keron Walsh family.
> "The good family deserves your prayers and your help in this time of trouble."

The notice also alerted everyone to the symptoms of polio: "Headache, nausea, vomiting, muscle soreness or stiffness, stiff neck, fever, nasal voice and difficulty in swallowing. In case of any of these symptoms the patient should be confined to bed and the family physician should be called at once."

The day was still young when Dr. Leonard decided Julie should be taken to St. Anthony's and tested for polio. He said Julie had an odd case in which she developed symptoms several days earlier, appeared to be recovering and then developed symptoms again.

Julie well remembered going with Mom and Dad to St. Anthony's emergency room where they were met by Dr. Leonard.

"I remember how dark and cold the emergency room seemed and of how scared I was that I, too, might have polio. I was asked to lie on my side and curl up like a ball with my knees under my chin while a needle was put into my spinal canal to withdraw the fluid to be checked for evidence of polio. The test results were positive — I had polio."

Once again Mom and Dad drove to Township Hospital, delivering Julie to the nurses.

Once again they waited until the nurses brought them another brown paper bag, this one with Julie's clothes inside. She was put in a room close to the ward where Ed had joined Dave. The whooshing sound of Dave's iron lung was Julie's constant companion.

Before attending Tuesday night's service at St. Mary's, Mom checked with Dr. Leonard to see about Dave's condition. The doctor said Dave was very ill but she might help him and all of us best by attending the service.

Except for the two front pews, St. Mary's was jammed, with people standing in the back of the church and half-way up the two outside aisles. A large crowd also attended a prayer service at the Methodist Church. Earlier that day, Dave's classmates held a special prayer meeting for him.

Midway through the St. Mary's service, Mom felt a tap on her shoulder. Both Dave and Ed had taken a turn for the worse — "they were not expected to survive the night," Mom said — and she and Dad were needed at the hospital.

"When we arrived at the hospital, authorities invited us into the isolation area, where we were given a room and asked to stay all night," Mom said. "The priest was called from St. Peter's again and both Dave and Ed were anointed and given the last rites.

"Ed was placed in an iron lung that night and Dave was packed in ice in his iron lung — his temperature kept rising. When we entered his room the sight we beheld was beyond words. The huffing of the iron lung, the suction machine, the flushed face and wild eyes of our once happy and spirited young men almost caused me to faint.

"The hushed voices of the nurses and the concern on their faces told us what we dare not ask.

"We were asked to come to a room where a young priest was

waiting to offer us comfort and spiritual quotations, speaking highly of our sons who seemed to be such brave wonderful boys — a credit to their parents. After the priest left, we were taken to a room where two beds were made up for us. We lay down, but this was not a night for sleeping."

They stayed the night and arose to find the condition of the boys unchanged. Before returning home, "we felt we must go to Rose's bedside," Mom said. "She was now going through rigorous physiotherapy with hot packs several times a day. She was still very weak, lying so still with sandbags still in place."

Before leaving Mom and Dad were told to avoid any financial transactions that would incur expenses because treating polio would be costly, much more than $25,000. They were told to engage three private duty nurses for each of us in the hospital.

When they arrived home, "the farmyard was crowded with cars of neighbors who had come to do chores, religious groups who had come to pray, health authorities and relatives who had come to offer words of comfort and hope and newspaper men," Mom said.

The news media had become "the biggest problem in trying to get the chores done," said Ken Krienke, a neighbor who often did our chores. "They would be there morning and evening and follow around whomever was working outside…they were like hounds. They wanted a story and were bound to get it one way or the other."

Within hours after Mom and Dad arrived home, Dave and Ed's conditions improved and the crisis eased.

Julie's first full day at Township, on Wednesday, Sept. 14, was anything but comfortable and quiet. The hospital had no air conditioning so the summer heat that continued into September was overpowering. Even with the single window in her room open, the hot, humid air seemed frozen in place. Making matters worse was the repair work on the parking lot just outside Julie's window. The smell of the tar made her nauseated and gave her headaches.

52

The next day, on Thursday, Sept. 15, Joan's symptoms worsened and Dr. Leonard ordered a spinal tap for her at St. Anthony's. Polio was confirmed.

Once again Mom and Dad drove to Township Hospital, delivering Joan to the nurses.

Once again they waited until the nurses brought them a fifth brown paper bag, this one containing Joan's clothes.

"She developed a rigid back…and became listless," Dr. Leonard said. "We moved her when she didn't show signs of improvement so she can be closely watched." He termed her condition as "good."

Joan was placed in Julie's room—the twins were now roommates. The nurses kidded Joan that she would do anything to be with her twin.

Thus in the course of seven days, Mom and Dad had endured an unimaginable crisis: four more children hospitalized with polio, two placed in iron lungs, two episodes requiring emergency treatment to keep their oldest sons alive and the quarantine of all their children at home.

"The hard-working, deeply religious farm couple showed the terrific strain they have experienced since Rose was admitted to the hospital two weeks earlier," a story on Sept. 18 on Page One of *The Rockford Morning Star* said. "Faith in God kept the family united."

"If we don't have God and religion, we don't have anything," Dad said.

"It's just like a whirlwind," Mom said. "We were swept into it fast and haven't had a chance to settle down and realize just what's going on."

"Everybody has stuck with us fine so far," Dad added. "If it keeps up I'm sure everything will come out all right."

The offers of support, financial and moral, were increasing daily from as far away as California. A woman from Los Angeles telephoned to say she was praying for all of us and asked what more she could do.

"I just told her to keep praying," Dad said. "We need all the prayers we can get."

Little did he realize that our family was about to be smothered with hundreds of thousands of prayers and an outpouring of financial assistance.

Rose at St. Anthony's Hospital in Rockford in September 1955. (The Rockford Morning Star).

Dad and Mom with Tom, left, and Bernie on the front doorstep in September 1955. (WREX-TV).

54

Mr. and Mrs. Maurice Murphy, at right, bringing us food in September 1955. From left are Aunt Margaret, Lorraine and Aunt Daisy. (WREX-TV).

Our sisters — from left: Joan, Anne, Alice and Sue — looking out the front window of our farmhouse in September 1955. (WREX-TV).

Friends and neighbors attend a prayer service for our family at St. Mary Catholic Church on Sept. 13, 1955. This photo, taken by Roger DeWert for WREX-TV, was published on Sept. 26 in Life magazine. In the front row at center is Mike Waller. To his far right is his brother Steve, his mother Esther, and a buddy, Mo Ostergard. (WREX-TV/Roger DeWert).

Martina Hines, right, with Florence Graham (left) and Mary Graham at the St. Mary's prayer service. (WREX-TV).

CHAPTER 7:

"Strike It Rich"

One evening during this hectic week while parking their car at Township Hospital Mom and Dad were met by two men from WREX-TV, program manager Jack Mazie and general manager Joe Baisch. They urged our parents to appear on the CBS-TV game show "Strike It Rich."

The 30-minute show hosted by Warren Hull was telecast every weekday morning live from CBS studios in New York City. It featured contestants who often were in need of funds to pay medical bills. They were awarded $500 if they could answer four questions.

At first Dad declined the offer.

"He's a proud man," Father Driscoll told a reporter. "He's not looking for money. He wants prayers."

After much discussion, Dad agreed, but only if the show would be treated as an extension of the "call to prayer" carried on all week at Durand churches. However, Mom and Dad would not leave our sick brothers and sisters to go to New York. So Lorraine, Aunt Margaret and Father Driscoll were chosen to appear Friday, Sept. 16, on the show. WREX's Mazie accompanied them on the trip.

Preparations began at once. Baisch and Robert B. Selfridge, manager of the Greater Rockford airport, arranged with Ken Zimmerman of Sterling, Ill., president of Illini Airlines, to fly the trio gratis from Rockford to Chicago. Zimmerman himself volunteered to be the pilot and enlisted co-pilot George Keith. American Airlines picked up the cost of the flight from Chicago to New York and back.

Lorraine was a reluctant participant. "It was the last thing I wanted to do," she said. "I had never flown before and was scared to death."

She packed her charcoal wool suit she had made for the 4-H fair and a hat from our cousin Mary Lou's collection of more than 100. Mary Lou also borrowed Marge McCorkle's shoes for Lorraine to wear.

The press turned out in full force at the Rockford Airport for the flight to Chicago.

"She managed to smile for photographers but her face indicated her thoughts were in Rockford Township Hospital, where iron lungs are pumping life into her brothers, Dave, 17 and Edward, 16, victims of bulbar polio," wrote Roger Hedges of *The Rockford Morning Star*. "Both are in critical condition and are being fed through tubes."

"I'm certainly going to take the opportunity to thank everybody for being so wonderful," Aunt Margaret told the reporters.

At the same time, Dr. Leonard declared that Julie "is having a rough time and may be heading for trouble as she enters the advanced stages of spinal polio."

The departure at 3:45 p.m. of Lorraine, Aunt Margaret and Father Driscoll came as E. Kenneth Todd, publisher of the *Morning Star* and *Rockford Register-Republic*, announced the establishment of a fund drive for our family with a $250 contribution from the newspapers. G. Arthur Johnson, Dad's friend and neighbor and vice president of Rockford's Central National Bank, was put in charge of the fund. Any money collected not needed for us would be turned over to the Winnebago County chapter of the National Foundation of Infantile Paralysis.

Upon landing at Midway Airport in Chicago, Lorraine was startled to discover she was being paged. "We thought for sure that Dave and Ed had passed away," Lorraine said. But it was only more reporters wanting to ask her questions.

They flew out for New York. Aunt Margaret, who had never flown before, remembered flying over Pittsburgh and seeing the fires from the steel mills. Father Driscoll, Brooklyn born and raised, was an old hand at flying.

After landing in New York, where it was very hot, they were escorted to the Prince George Hotel, on East 28th Street between 5th Avenue and Madison Avenue. It was built in 1904. In 1955 and for years it was one of the city's premier hotels. But it eventually fell into disrepair and was renovated in 1999, when it was reopened as a home for homeless and low-income people.

Lorraine's first task upon checking in to the hotel was to write a note to Rose on an American Airlines postcard. It read:

> *"Dear Rose Ellen,*
>
> *"I am sending this card to you from New York. Aunt Margaret, Father Driscoll and I are in New York to be on 'Strike It Rich.' We flew in on a big airplane, just like the ones that go over our place.*
> *"Love,*
> *Lorraine"*

Later in the day, Father Driscoll knocked on the women's door and invited them to go down to the lobby for a cold drink. "I got an iced tea," Aunt Margaret said.

The next morning, another escort arrived and accompanied them to the CBS studios for their appearance on "Strike It Rich."

After preliminary greetings, Father Driscoll told the host, Warren Hull, that our family needed the prayers of everyone. He asked that the prayers from all over the nation be united with ours and those of people in the Durand area.

Hull asked the audience to join in a moment of silent prayer. As Lorraine, Aunt Margaret and Father Driscoll got ready to answer the game-show questions, Hull announced that the $500 prize was being awarded to Lorraine outright — there would be no questions.

Before the program ended, the studio was flooded with calls asking for our address so that the callers could send money. Lorraine, Aunt Margaret and Father Driscoll thanked everyone for their help and Hull wrapped up the program on an upbeat note.

In Durand, the town had shut down as friends and neighbors gathered around television sets to watch the nationwide appeal.

"Everything was closed down tight," said Lloyd Heinen, telegraph agent at the Chicago, Milwaukee and St. Paul railroad depot in town. "You couldn't get as much as a loaf of bread." Even farmers came in from the fields to watch the show. Bob Vormezeele and Uncle Laurence stopped their combines in Dad's field of red clover and went to the house to watch. Time out also was taken at St. Rose's Priory in Dubuque, Ia., so that the show could be seen by Aunt Margaret's son, Jerry, and his colleagues, who were studying for the priesthood.

Julie watched the television show from her hospital bed. A set was placed outside the double glass doors of the contagion ward. Dave's nurses watched part of the show, then went into his room to relate the details to him. Ed was sleeping.

At the high school, Supt. Paul G. Norsworthy arranged for a television set to be hooked up in Study Hall, which was jammed with students and teachers. You couldn't see much from the back of the room, but you could hear the show — the room was so quiet you could hear mice racing in the walls.

Years later, nearly everyone remembered watching "Strike It Rich," though the details had faded for most.

After the show ended, another escort was waiting to accompany Lorraine, Aunt Margaret and Father Driscoll back to the airport. They bought a *New York Times*, which featured a photograph of Mom, Tom and Bernie. "It brought tears to our eyes," said Aunt Margaret. They phoned home to find out the latest condition of all of us in the hospital.

"No change" was the answer. Within hours they flew to Chicago and were driven back to Rockford, arriving about 8 p.m.

A battery of reporters was waiting for them.

Lorraine and Father Driscoll said the dramatic nationwide appeal for prayers was successful.

"I'm sure it did a lot of good," Lorraine said. "Everybody has been so wonderful. I just don't know what to say."

"We told those people it was prayers we wanted, and they went right along with us," Father Driscoll said. "The show was just what we wanted."

"I hope we thanked everyone enough," added Aunt Margaret. "We ran out of time on the television show and I wanted to say how much we appreciate everyone's prayers and help."

Lorraine noted that it was long past visiting hours and she would have to wait until the next morning to see her brothers and sisters at the hospital.

Meanwhile, the special fund set up for our family only hours earlier swelled quickly. Bob Clyde, the news director at WREX-TV, estimated that contributions had topped $1,000 in the first day. Art Johnson, the fund's custodian and vice president of Central National Bank, said another $305 was given to him in the bank "by people who were just passing by."

Office space at the bank was limited, "so a small cloakroom adjoining the men's restroom was used as a counting room for contributions," said Bill Smith, an assistant to Art Johnson. "An old dining-room table and folding chairs served as a place where family and friends, all ladies as I recall, gathered to open envelopes and to separate check, currency, coin and written notes of concern. I believe this act of genuine love for the Walsh family was performed for several weeks, but not every day of the week."

Among the women counting the contributions were Aunt Margaret, Caroline Johnson, Art's wife, Dad's sister Aunt Agnes Carroll and her daughter Rosemary Richardson, Hazel Gaffney and Virginia and Ruth Flynn, from St. Patrick's Catholic Church in Irish Grove.

Summing up the day was an editorial from a publication whose identity has been lost to time. It said, in part:

"Americans need not to be told what to do when misfortune strikes friends, neighbors and kinfolk, whether they live nearby or far away. The courageous fight of the polio sufferers, the parents' determination to see it through, the devoted ministry of the family physician and parish priest, and the pictures of the children's friends and playmates kneeling in prayer have touched the nation's heart."

The front page of The Rockford Morning Star on Sept. 17, 1955.

Cousin Mary Lou Walsh, who gave one of her many hats to Lorraine to wear on her trip to "Strike It Rich." (Walsh family photo).

Lorraine, left, Aunt Margaret and Father Driscoll at Midway Airport in Chicago on Sept. 15, 1955 on their way to New York to appear on the "Strike It Rich" television show. (Photo source unknown).

CHAPTER 8:

Cards, Letters and Visitors

As Dave and Ed's condition continued to slowly improve, newspaper reports began painting a picture of a brighter outlook. "We're greatly encouraged, even though there is a great deal of anxiety about our children," Dad said.

Some of that anxiety was directed at our little sister Fran, who was at home dealing with a light case of polio. Her neck muscles were weak but "she finally recovered after immersing her in a tub of hot water several times a day for several days," Mom said.

Despite the optimism of the press, the reality was that our family was still in the middle of a one-family polio epidemic. Mom and Dad were still making at least two trips a day to Rockford to visit their sick children and there were at least nine mouths to feed at our dinner table three times a day.

Nevertheless, Dad granted a reporter from *The Chicago Herald-American* an interview and tour of our farm.

"Everybody tells us, 'don't be afraid to holler when you need help,'" Dad said. "And Art Johnson — he's our neighbor and vice president of the bank in Rockford — told us: 'Don't worry. If you need money we'll take care of it.'"

Dad walked reporter Edwin Diamond around the farm, stopping in the barn where two of his nephews who had farms and families of their own were milking the cows. "They weren't asked to, but they came over and pitched in," Dad said. "We're getting their prayers, too. And that's important. Father Driscoll of our parish is saying rosaries for us.

And the Methodists held prayer meetings, too."

Back at the parish house in town, Father Driscoll extolled our family: "These are the kind of people that make America great. There is no delinquency or hate here. Sure we have our problems but not from the Walshes — altar boys, honor students. That's the kind of family it is."

Optimism prevailed at the hospitals. At St. Anthony's, Rose was sitting up and talking cheerily for the first time since becoming ill. At Township Hospital, Dr. Leonard reported that Dave had "improved quite a bit but is still far from well." Dad said treatments for Dave "might stretch out for a long time. He was so bad the other night the doctor gave up on him." Dr. Leonard said Ed had rallied and fought off throat paralysis.

Mom and Dad still could talk to them only briefly. Dave wanted to hear all the details of Lorraine's trip to New York and "Strike It Rich."

Joan and Julie were feeling much better, good enough to listen as Mom read letters to them from friends, relatives and strangers. *The Rockford Morning Star* published a photograph of Julie listing her age as 17, not 13. As a result, she got letters from lots of potential suitors.

Since the "Strike It Rich" telecast, the cards and letters began pouring in from all over the country and world, including some from South Korea, Japan, Switzerland, Canada, France and Germany. There were so many that mailman Floyd "Bump" Sarver delivered them to our house in a wooden clothes basket nearly every day for weeks.

Many of the letters misspelled our name and had weird addresses on the envelope. Dad's name, Keron, was spelled in more than a dozen different ways: Karen, Kernon, Kerran, Karren, Karow, Karm, Kerin and Karon. Our family name was spelled Walch, Welch, Halek, Waltc, Waltz, Waalsh and Wash. Durand was often misspelled Durant, Duran, Durante and Duront. Wrong addresses included "The Walsh Family, 4 miles north of Durand, IL" and "RR, 5 miles south of Wisconsin border." One letter's address read: "To the man & and wife who have those 8 children with polio. Please give this letter to them."

Many of the cards and letters contained money and all of them conveyed the prayers and best wishes of the sender. Donations included many envelopes with just a dollar. Some had coins, such as two quarters or four FDR dimes, taped to the notes.

Some letters recommended how we should treat polio.

From Hotchkiss, Colo: "…warm up some lard and add 2 to 3 drops turpentine to a teaspoon and rub in skin on all body and cover with flannel…and you will see your whole family get completely well."

From Great Falls, Mont.: "rye bread, mush and rye-crisp all taken with fruit…no one child or anyone will have polio if they live on rye bread."

The first card we received came from Mr. and Mrs. Alfred Alberica of Rutland, Vermont, the first area in the United States to have a polio epidemic, in the late 1890s.

Other letters came:

From Bucks County, Pennsylvania to Mom and Dad: "While listening to Dick Clark's Caravan of music this afternoon on the radio, he told his listeners about your misfortune—that you have nine children stricken with polio within the last ten days. May God give you strength and courage to face the heartache which you must feel at this time and I pray that the outcome may be all that you wish…yours in faith," Mrs. R. L. Andress.

From an Army Base in Japan to Mom and Dad: "You all will be surprised to be hearing from a G.I. that you don't even know…I don't know why I am writing. I guess it is because I have lost so many of my own people to polio…if there is anything I could do I would like to know," Tony Campbell.

From a woman in Moultrie, Ga. to Bernie and Tom: "I have been reading in the papers about your brothers and sisters having polio and how smart you two boys are in helping your aunt with the housework, so I am sending you twenty-five dollars each to buy some school clothes, for I know it takes all of your father's money for your sick brothers and sisters…," Mrs. Jim Holmes.

From the Rockford Deanery President of the National Council of Catholic Women to Mom and Dad: "This is no doubt the hardest letter I have ever written. At a time like this words fail one, but sincerely you and yours have been in my thoughts and prayers…As president of the Rockford Deanery Council of the N.C.C.W., of which St. Mary's of Durand is affiliated…I have written each and every one of the affiliated parish presidents, of which there are nineteen, to offer their opening or closing prayers at their next monthly meeting for your intention…have faith, all will come out in the end…May God bless you in your trials and tribulations, sincerely," Florence (Mrs. Wm.) Stralow.

From Montreal to Mom and Dad: "Here in Montreal we have great faith and devotion to our Mother of Perpetual Help and I enclose the only picture I have, and some rice pictures—which can be swallowed with a drink of water…which I am sure will help your children…, sincerely," M. M.

From Naugatuck, Conn., to Mom and Dad: "We have a seven-month-old daughter who is dying with progressive muscular atrophy, a disease with no known cure. Money can't help her, so we would like to try and help you, although two dollars isn't very much," Mrs. John Moruska.

From Newton, Mass., to the Walsh family: "The Walsh family has been enrolled for one year by John and Ruth Walsh (no relation to our family) to share the Spiritual Benefits of 350 Masses said, 1,000 Masses heard, 1,500 Rosaries and 15,000 prayers. Together with the graces from the Missionary Activities of the Jesuit Father, the Native Sisters and the good works of the Faithful of their Mission in Jamaica."

From a Philadelphia Prison inmate to Julie: "Just a little letter to say hello and I hope you are getting along fine. I also hope you have received all my cards I have sent you as I know a letter sometimes is a great help…by the way, Julie, I hope that if there is anything you need I'll be glad to have it sent to you…, God bless you and best regards,"

Anthony Deleonardo.

From Springfield, Mo., to Julie: "I saw your picture and thought you were pretty…I am 6 feet tall, weigh 175, have blond curly hair and light green eyes…Hope you get well soon…, With love," Merrill.

From Brooklyn, N.Y., to Julie: "It seems strange that an attractive girl like you has been stricken with a bad disease. Try not to let it bother you. Before I saw your beautiful face I was reading the Bible… my address is below, please give me yours…," Barry.

From LaPorte City, Ind., to Joan and Julie: "I've been reading about you in the paper and thought maybe you'd be pleased to get a card or letter. If you would like to have a pen pal, I'd be very glad to write (either one or both)…God bless you all," Betty Bertsch. "P.S. I'll say some prayers for you, too."

Many of our family members wrote to all of us, filling us in on the latest news and encouraging us in our battle to recover.

From our Grandpa Kenucane to Dave: "Keep up your courage. It won't be long before your great trial will be over with. Remember, we are all praying for you."

From Aunt Teresa (Mom's sister Teresa Houghton, a registered nurse) to Ed: "Just gain a little each day and when it's added up, it will be complete recovery."

From Aunt Pat (Mom's sister Pat Kenucane) to Dave: "Hello David. Keep your Irish chin up, fellow, just like you have…And I know you know how Eddie is, so I can't tell you much about him…From what I hear about Ed's voice, he must be able to talk to you anywhere in the hospital. Father Driscoll swears that when Ed says "Hi Father" you can hear it in Durand…I hear you had a letter from Eddie Matthews (Milwaukee Braves star third baseman). That ought to make a few people jealous. Wasn't that nice of him?"

From Aunt Mary (Mom's sister Mary Mulcahy) to Ed: "Max is picking corn, trying to beat the 45 snowstorms predicted this winter by the man in Brodhead. I would love to be your English tutor when you're feeling better."

From Mary Lou Walsh to Dave: "I know you heard about Dad getting a new Ford. Pheasant season opens in about an hour. They had a dance at the Grange (in Durand) last night for you. They made $175. I didn't go. I'm kinda on the loose now…maybe you can take care of an old maid cousin when you get back or find someone for me."

From our sister Anne Walsh to Dave: "Bob (Walsh), Joe (Walsh) and Dick Johnson did the milking today. They got done about 5 p.m…. Marilyn (Waller) and Jack (Graham) are getting married in June…we are going to say the rosary now. I will have to close."

Praying the rosary at home was a nightly event.

"One evening while we were on our knees, we heard a knock on the door," Julie recalled. "Dad got up to answer it and was greeted by a man who told him he could heal our family if Dad let him come into the house. Dad told him he could come in only if he wanted to kneel and pray the rosary with us. The man left immediately and we finished praying."

Many of our classmates and friends wrote often, reporting on the latest news and gossip at school.

From the Kelsey family to all of us: "Dear neighbors, you have such a lovely family. It just doesn't seem right that you have been hit so hard…hoping with all our hearts. Your anxious neighbors," the Kelsey family. "P.S. Lorraine looked so lovely on TV."

From Dave's classmate and cousin Jack Walsh to Dave and Ed: "Your old buddies are coming down to see you in a couple of days. We have been talking to your mother and she said it would be better to wait a couple of days until Dave would have more strength…the sophomores are having a roller skating party. Marilee Keller invited me. Hope you've got some good-looking nurses to make things interesting."

From Jack Walsh to Dave: "This has been the busiest week at school yet. We had a class meeting today and it was just like they always are, fighting and chewing about one thing all period. We started selling ads for the annual (yearbook) last week and we got $200 already…The new Chevys are coming out tomorrow. We have a beautiful bronze and cream 205 h.p. and a gray and white 210 h.p. for the showing…I'll try and send you some literature on the cars next week…Mom and Dad said to say 'hello.' Jerry Sarver is going steady with Kay G. now. Never thought of that, did you?…You keep giving her all you got to try and get better and I'll do my share of praying."

From Dave's classmate and cousin Bob Haggerty: "P.G. (School Supt. Paul G. Norsworthy) said we couldn't have taverns in the annual ads. He really blew when he saw them. See you big boy!"

From Ed's classmate Dan McCullough to Dave: "Danny Waller sends you a card every day. That makes up for me missing you by at least a month."

From Julie's best friend and classmate, Jean Rafferty, to Julie and Joan: "Anne and Alice came to school today and said we should write, so here goes. I've got the best piece of news!! Corky Cuthbertson saw (two high school teachers) in this car on the road on which Dixons used to live, and they were necking!!!! We had the worst dinner at school today. It was stew, and I think it had liver in it. Ugh! … Eugene sits in algebra and tells Nancy J. he loves her. Oh Brother! P.S. We picked secret sisters in F.H.A. I got Nancy Greene. (Thank Goodness)."

From an unnamed student in Study Hall to Dave and Ed: "I'm writing this in Study Hall…Jack Walsh and some boys are playing cards…somebody is shooting water pistols and I'm getting wet."

A clever card was sent to Ed from his classmates Dan and Dave McCullough, twin brothers. Dan wrote: "It was good to see you and Dave again last night. Dave looks better every time I see him. I hope you both keep it up and you will be out of there in no time."

On the blank inside of the card, Dave McCullough offered his creative touch. He drew a picture of Ed in an iron lung entitled "Coming Attraction Soon to Be Seen at Winnebago County Hospital."

The drawing showed three nurses and some of Ed's high school classmates working with a wrecking bar, sledge hammer, wedge, dynamite and a "church key" to free him from his iron lung.

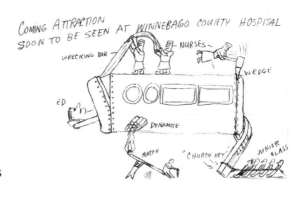

Nearly as many visitors as letters showed up at Township Hospital to see both Dave and Ed.

In addition to immediate family members who visited every day, Dave's classmates Jack Walsh, Bob Haggerty, Tom Dolan and Norm Chilton visited almost as often, even though they were scared they were going to be next to get polio. Jack went to Mass almost daily to pray for Dave and Ed and also to pray that he wouldn't get sick. The other Dolan cousins — Mary, Mike and Charlotte — also visited frequently.

For many visitors, seeing Dave and Ed in iron lungs was a shock. "It broke our hearts and made us cry," said Dave's classmate Karen Holland. Teacher Harry Vale and his wife Cres were stunned and felt especially sad on their first visit. Louis Thomas, owner with Al McCartney of the Standard Service Station one mile south of Durand, worried constantly about the boys and visited them often. Others, such as Bill Flynn, felt Dave and Ed had great attitudes, were always happy and never gave up. Bill was sure both would recover.

Other frequent visitors included Dave's classmates Don Waller, Sally Stetler and Dan Waller and Ed's classmates Dave and Dan McCullough, Jerry Engelbrecht and Bev Meier, with her boyfriend Ken Waller. "We never forgot Dave and Ed," Bev said. "They remained part of our group wherever they were."

Joan and Julie's visitors were mostly family members and Father Driscoll since their school friends were too young to drive. A *Rockford*

Morning Star reporter stopped by to interview Julie and asked about her favorite movie star. Ann Blyth, said Julie. Not long afterward, a special delivery package arrived with a hand-written letter from Ann Blyth along with a beautiful pale blue bed jacket with fine, fluffy feathers for trim. The reporter had contacted the actress.

At the same time, hundreds of relatives, friends and neighbors were busy helping our family. Many continued daily prayers for us and every night some drove to the farm with home-cooked dinners. Some cousins and neighbors showed up in the morning and evening to help with the daily chores.

Most prominent was Ken Krienke, who worked at the Miller Vault Company in Durand and lived with his wife Bonnie in the cheese factory at Baker and Wheeler roads. Many people helped with the chores but none so often as Ken; he came several times a week for several months.

On Monday, Sept. 19, the "Strike It Rich" telecast of Lorraine, Aunt Margaret and Father Driscoll was rebroadcast on the radio, prompting another spurt of contributions to the fund drive for our family. The total jumped to $3,838 by Wednesday and to $4,186 by Friday. It included $9.16 from eight youngsters from Freeport, Ill., who staged a backyard circus for the Red Cross. When they learned the Red Cross had met its quota, they gave the money to our fund. Other contributions came from as far away as Los Angeles. Realtor Marshall Taggart heard the show and sent a check for $20 with a note typed on business stationery.

That week was a special one for Joan and Julie. On Wednesday, Sept. 21, they were transferred from Rockford Township Hospital to St. Anthony's, where they remained roommates. They began intensive physical therapy the next day.

Father Driscoll visited them the day before at Township. He blessed them and told them he had been to our farm. "Everyone is fine and wanted to say hello," he told the girls. He then turned to Mrs.

Catherine McGinnis, the superintendent of nurses, and said: "Katie, I understand the girls' vacation here is about ended."

Mrs. McGinnis had returned early from her vacation to help care for our brothers and sisters. "I came from Durand," she said. "I know the family. You can imagine how I felt when I got a telegram about all this."

Joan and Julie's departure left only Dave and Ed at Township Hospital. Dave's condition, still very serious, improved to the point that he was able to be out of his iron lung two to three minutes about six times a day. Ed was out of his iron lung seven to eight minutes every hour.

His nurse, Mrs. Mary Burns, reported that "Eddie can read comic books attached by rubber bands to his respirator. We move him to the window and by looking in his mirror he can see everything going on way down the river. His voice has become very strong and, as Father Driscoll says, when Eddie sees you in the driveway and calls out, you can hear him all the way to Durand."

Dad and Mom open letters at home. Some of us can be seen in the mirror above their head. (Walsh family photo).

Some of us saying the rosary at home during our nightly prayer time in September 1955. From left are Tom, Bernie, Sue, Alice, Lorraine, Anne and Bill. (The Observer — Official Newspaper of the Catholic Diocese of Rockford).

Jean Rafferty, Julie's best friend who helped her win a trip to the State Fair. (Senior class photo).

CHAPTER 9:

Off to Chicago

Joan and Julie's room at St. Anthony's was next to the nurses' station, so they stopped in often to check on the girls. "We especially enjoyed the student nurses but were given wonderful care by all of them," Julie said. "It was during this time that I decided I wanted to be a nurse someday."

The physical therapy routine for Joan and Julie began each day with range-of-motion exercises and warm water exercises in the Hubbard Tank, a figure-eight shaped whirlpool-like container that gave the medical staff easy access to patients.

Therapy also included the application of warm woolen packs to their arms and legs. The wraps were called Sister Kenny Packs and, like the time in the Hubbard Tank, were designed to loosen and soothe sore muscles prior to stretching exercises. Both girls said the smell of the wet wool was unforgettable, not offensive but distinctive, like the smell of wet woolen mittens.

"One of our therapists also worked with Rose and kept us up to date about how she was doing." Julie said. "That therapist loved our little sister."

Rose's treatments were similar.

She was "bathed in bed and her muscles gently massaged during the bath," said Carol Sciame, a student nurse. "The nurses put Sister Kenny packs on her arms, legs and back." Despite all this, added Ms. Sciame, Rose "was always a happy little girl."

The coverage of our polio ordeal continued in newspapers

throughout the country and even in *Life* magazine and *Newsweek*. On Sept. 26, *Life* published a photograph of one of the services at St. Mary's Church for our family, showing people kneeling in prayer. On the same day, *Newsweek* published a small story about us.

On Sept. 29, several newspapers reported that 10 in our family had been stricken to some degree with polio.

"Dr. Leonard said he has found 'some weakness' in five of the nine children at home while five others are hospitalized," *The Rockford Register-Republic* reported. None of the reports, however, named the five at home.

To this day, none of us is certain how many of us came down with polio. Most likely, the number is 11.

The five most serious cases were Rose, Dave, Ed, Joan and Julie, all of whom were hospitalized. The other six cases were diagnosed by Dr. Leonard at our home. He based his diagnosis on his exams and symptoms he observed as well as symptoms reported by Mom. These ranged from very, very mild with some slight leg weakness (Bill, Bernie — despite his vaccination — and Tom) to very mild, having just a stiff neck (Sue), to mild, being in bed with a headache and stiff neck, "just not feeling good" (Anne) and noticeable muscle weakness (Fran). Not stricken were Lorraine, Alice and Molly. Some newspapers reported that Mom and Dad also were stricken with mild cases. But those reports were mistaken; Mom and Dad never contracted polio.

October opened with a rush of optimistic news reports. Dr. Leonard announced that Dave would be transferred in the next few weeks to the Illinois Research Respiratory Center in Chicago. The doctor said it did not indicate any worsening of Dave's condition. Rather, he said, the center was set up to handle the state's most difficult respiratory cases and had equipment that would make it possible for Dave to continue breathing while out of his iron lung for therapy.

Dave's condition continued to improve and his diet was expanded to include gelatin and egg nog, according to Dr. Leonard. As usual,

Dave was fed through a tube. He was unable to breathe outside of his iron lung but Ed was now able to spend three hours a day out of his iron lung. Dr. Leonard said Ed had some paralysis in his arms, legs and chest but his ability to breathe unassisted was slowly returning.

Dr. Leonard also announced that Joan and Julie would be released in the next few days from St. Anthony's "if the family is able to handle them at home." They would have to return periodically to the hospital for treatments. Rose was "coming along very well," Dr. Leonard said, but would have to remain in the hospital for at least another month.

On Oct. 3, the doctor also lifted the quarantine for six of us at home. Before releasing us, he had all of us undergo thorough physical therapy evaluations at St. Anthony's. Early the next morning the school bus came to pick up Anne and Alice, sophomores, Sue, seventh grade, Bill, sixth grade, Bernie, third grade, and Tom, first grade. Parties planned by classmates greeted all of them.

Meanwhile, the fund for our family topped $7,500, with a large contribution of $700 coming from employees of the Yates American machine company in Beloit, Wis., where Aunt Pat Kenucane worked as secretary to the president and chairman. In addition, the chairman of the company, Edward J. Dalton, gave an anonymous gift of $1,000. Another significant contribution of $130 was raised after promoter and Winnebago County Deputy Sheriff Joe Ferona organized a professional wrestling benefit match highlighting Canadian champion Roy McClarity. He appeared with popular wrestling star Lorraine Johnson at Harlem High School in Rockford.

On Saturday, Oct. 8, Joan and Julie returned home as scheduled. Ed's condition continued to improve and he was now using a rocking bed and chest respirator during the daytime, staying in the iron lung only at night.

Friends and neighbors continued to drop by our farm with food. Many brought fresh vegetables from their gardens as well as fully cooked meals for everyone. Nearly every morning and night someone showed up to help with the chores.

One morning, several of them arrived at our farm for an old-fashioned "corn-picking bee." Bill had just boarded the school bus that day, Oct. 20, when he saw a parade of farmers with corn pickers and other equipment rolling down the hill on Baker Road to help Dad pick his corn

"I just wanted to stay home and help that day," said Bill, then 10 years old, who in the past few weeks had become one of "the men" helping with the chores. But he remained on the bus and went to school, hoping that the men might still be there when he got home.

The more than 60 friends and neighbors who came to pick the 65 acres of corn on our 360-acre farm were mostly from Laona Township and St. Mary's parish. They were led by Merle Anderson, the Illinois state representative from Laona Township, and Maurice McMahon, commander of the Durand American Legion Post.

They brought 14 two-row corn pickers, 20 tractors and 34 wagons. Some of the wagons weren't in the best of shape, prompting Uncle Laurence to declare the line-up "looks like the grapes of wrath!" Mom and Dad watched the troops deploy, including our cousin Marian Walsh driving Dad's corn picker. Joan and Julie were allowed to be outside a short while to watch the action.

Our neighbor Bob Dobler brought his movie camera and used it often. Years later Bill recalled Bob showing the movie at our house. It captured the men bringing in the corn and then Bob ran it in reverse to show corn jumping out of the crib and back into the field.

The job was finished by noon. The men harvested nearly 4,000 bushels of corn in 3 ½ hours and then walked the short distance to Aunt Daisy's house where 15 women from St. Anne's Sodality of St. Mary's Church served lunch.

A photograph published the next day in *The Beloit Daily News* showed some of the men who helped with the harvest: Bob Navis, Joe

Walsh, Jim Walsh, Dad, Bob Dobler, Julius Englebrecht, Merle Meinert, Ray Englebretson, Bob Walsh, Joe Hines, Jon Dixon, Dick Johnson, Joe Gaffney, Mead Slocum and Leonard Walsh. Others helping but not in the photograph were Chuck Saelens, Ken Krienke and Otto Swale.

Aunt Mary visited Dave that same day and wrote to him that evening. "I hurried home as I wanted to watch TV at 5 to see the corn-picking pictures," she said. "They were just coming on and they were real good…Teresa and I thought you looked good and you're certainly doing wonderful…she thinks you will do well in Chicago."

Finally, Oct. 27, moving day for Dave, arrived.

His departure from Rockford Township Hospital to the Illinois Research Hospital in Chicago would allow doctors to keep him out of the iron lung long enough to enable them to massage life back into his arm and leg muscles. Dave had been in the iron lung more than a month, had lost his ability to swallow and had been out of the device for therapy for only minutes at a time.

The farewell was tearful for Mom and Dad but at times festive. All the nurses who cared for him at Township Hospital stopped by to say goodbye. Also on hand were Clarence Kleckner, chairman of the Winnebago County chapter of the National Foundation for Infantile Paralysis, Doris McMillin, the group's executive secretary, Township Supervisor Charles F. Brown and Markham May, hospital administrator.

Mom, Dad and Aunt Teresa remained in the background, with Father Driscoll moving between them and Dave. Watching quietly but with rapt attention was Ed, who was out of his iron lung laying on a gurney to say goodbye to his brother.

In the center of activity was Dr. George A. Saxton, the young Chicago polio specialist who made the trip to Rockford to supervise Dave's transfer to a lightweight portable ventilator called a Portalung. It was made of aluminum, weighed only 150 pounds and was being used for the first time to transfer a polio patient any distance by ambulance.

Assisting Dr. Saxton was Dr. Leonard.

Dr. Saxton, assistant professor of medicine at the University of Illinois and senior physician of research education at the Chicago center, was constantly busy as he directed the transfer. In addition to moving Dave from one breathing device to another, the nasal tube entering his nose and reaching his esophagus had to be switched. So did the suction tube inserted through a small opening in his trachea.

Through the entire transfer Dave remained alert and composed. Although his voice was less than a whisper, he was able to compliment his mother on her new dress.

The ambulance was equipped with special batteries to keep the Portalung pumping as well as a direct pressure tube to pump air into Dave's mouth and directly into his lungs, forcing him to breathe from within. The direct pressure tube would be used in the Chicago hospital while Dave underwent therapy.

"Gee, this aluminum lung is a swell thing," Dave told reporters. More wonderful was the fact that doctors were expecting Dave would not have to use the Portalung while in Chicago.

"We'll use the positive pressure tube and feed air into his lungs through the opening in his neck," said Dr. Saxton, allowing him to lie in bed just as comfortable as if he were well and in bed at home.

The crowd of doctors, nurses, patients, relatives and friends was silent as the huge ambulance pulled away, beginning the two-hour trip to Illinois Research Hospital. Mom, torn by weeks of worrying and sleepless nights, turned away in tears. Dad dabbed at his eyes with a handkerchief, while standing tall by Mom's side. As the crowd began breaking up, Father Driscoll's booming voice broke the silence: "Don't worry now. He's going to be all right."

Making the return trip to Chicago in the ambulance was Dr. Saxton and Aunt Teresa, whose nursing skills made her a welcome addition. Mom and Dad followed in their own car.

The trip to Chicago, on Highway 20 through Belvidere, Marengo and Elgin, was uneventful as Dave slept most of the way. Mom and Dad met with Dave for several minutes shortly after he was admitted to the hospital.

A hospital spokesman told reporters that a special team was awaiting Dave's arrival and would begin treating him in every way possible. The team included polio specialists, physicians, surgeons, nurses, physical therapists, occupational therapists and social workers. It would be the most specialized treatment of polio available in 1955.

After making the trip to Chicago Research Hospital, Aunt Teresa wrote a letter that night to Ed.

> *"Dear Ed,*
> *"Well here we are in Chicago.*
> *"We stayed in this hotel tonight (the Rosemoor Hotel on Jackson Boulevard). We had joining rooms. I don't hear your mother and dad yet so I am dropping you this line while I am waiting.*
> *"That is some place Dave is in. He was real comfortable when we left him. He is in a rocking bed and he said it is much more comfortable than the lung.*
> *"Well, Ed, I'll let your folks tell you all about our trip.*
> *"See you soon.*
> *"Love, Aunt Teresa."*

The next day, Oct. 28, with no press or fanfare and only Mom and Dad present, Ed was transferred from Rockford Township Hospital to St. Anthony's Hospital.

The month ended with the fund for our family reaching $8,000.

Barb Walsh gives her husband, Jim Walsh, a drink of water as he takes a break from helping 60 area farmers pick our corn crop on Oct. 21, 1955. (WREX-TV).

*Mom looks through the ambulance window as Dave rests in a portable breathing device in the ambulance that transferred him on Oct. 27, 1955, from Rockford Township Hospital to Chicago's Illinois Research Hospital. (*The Rockford Morning Star*).*

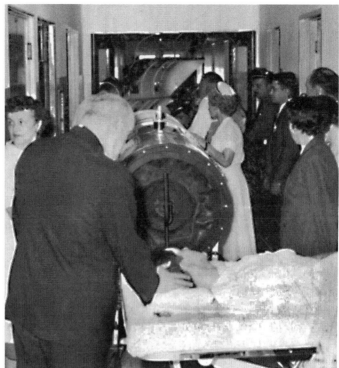

Father Driscoll pats Ed, out of his iron lung on a gurney watching Dave being prepared for his trip to Chicago. At left is nurse Marion Berg. (The Rockford Morning Star).

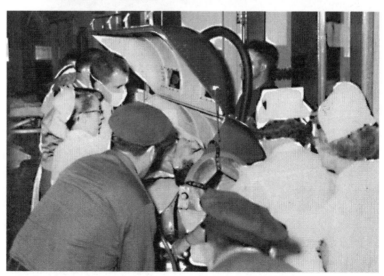

Dr. George A. Saxton, wearing face mask, helps Dave get ready for his trip to Chicago. Barely visible in the back left is Ed watching on a gurney. (The Rockford Morning Star).

83

David Walsh, Still Confined to Iron Lung, Is Taken to Chicago for New Treatment

The front page of The Rockford Morning Star *on Oct. 28 gives prominent coverage to Dave's transfer to Chicago.*

CHAPTER 10:

Much to Be Thankful For

As if coping with as many as 11 children with polio — two of them almost totally paralyzed — wasn't enough challenge for Mom and Dad, along came a new crisis.

It happened on Nov. 1, just after Dave had begun to settle in at the Illinois Research Hospital in Chicago and Ed had been transferred to St. Anthony's in Rockford.

"One night Dad and I were in charge of the household when Mother was in Chicago with Dave," Lorraine recalled. "Several of us were upstairs that evening when Fran and Molly started jumping on the beds. No one knew that 2-year-old Molly had manicure scissors in her hand when she fell into bed."

"We picked her up and checked her eye, which she said hurt a little bit," Julie said. "We couldn't see any obvious injury so we did not call the doctor."

Lorraine agreed.

"It didn't look too bad that night, but by morning it had swollen. We called Mom (in Chicago) and she met us at the eye doctor's office in Rockford."

Molly was hospitalized immediately; the little scissors had cut baby Molly's brown eye.

"Emergency surgery had to be done for repair of the laceration…," Julie said. "So she and Rose were now both patients in the pediatric unit at St. Anthony's.

"Mom told us that after surgery Molly's little arms had to be tied down in order for her not to touch her eye patch. It seemed so cruel knowing she could have no visitors except Mom and Dad and only briefly during visiting hours. Sister Grace continued to enforce the rigid rules.

"We prayed so hard that Molly would not lose vision in her eye and our prayers were answered."

Molly remembers the ophthalmologist leaning over her with a big silver circle on his head piece that had a bright light in the center. She spent a few days in the hospital and was sent home with dark sunglasses that wrapped around the side of her eyes to prevent any light from filtering in. She had frequent checkups for the next few months.

"Today the pupil in her injured eye has a most unusual shape," said Julie, "but her vision is OK."

Meanwhile, Dave continued to make progress in Chicago. He was now being removed from his iron lung for therapy and was responding "pretty well" to treatment for his weakened arms and legs, according to Dr. Leonard, who often visited Dave.

The doctor said polio specialists rigged a breathing device for Dave that eliminated the need for the iron lung and made therapy possible. Dave's body was so weakened from polio and his time in the iron lung that it was not yet possible to determine the extent of the crippling disease's effects.

More encouraging was Dave's renewed ability to swallow.

"He's swallowing three or four mouthfuls at a time now," Dr. Leonard said. "That's more than he was ever able to do in Rockford."

The doctor said Dave had adapted well to his new environment and was being cheered on by his roommate, a 24-year-old man whose condition was similar to Dave's when he entered the hospital. The roommate's improvement and good spirits were helpful to Dave, Dr. Leonard said.

Ed also continued to make progress.

He now spent about 16 hours a day on a rocking bed at St. Anthony's but continued to sleep at night in his iron lung.

Rose continued her treatment at St. Anthony's and was fitted with a corset to support her weakened abdominal muscles.

Barely a day passed when Dave didn't have visitors from our family. Mom visited the most, often riding the train from Rockford to Chicago and staying at the YWCA. Her sisters, especially Aunt Teresa who was a nurse, good friend Bernice Carroll and our cousin Mary Lou Walsh, often accompanied her. At times all of us took turns going with her.

Once, Bill joined Mom on the train. On the way home the train hit a car and someone was killed. Mom and Bill didn't get home until 2 o'clock in the morning.

Dr. Janet Wolter, the assistant director of the polio section at Research Hospital, developed a close personal relationship with our parents, offering support and comfort. The doctor remembered Dave as being very intelligent and never depressed by his condition. It wasn't long before she offered Mom the use of her apartment for Mom's extended visits to the hospital. The apartment was close and very convenient for Mom. Dr. Wolter stayed with her parents in their home in the suburbs when Mom used her apartment.

From the beginning, Dave also had lots of friends visit him in Chicago. Nine members of the newly formed high school Letterman's Club attended a Chicago Bears-Los Angeles Rams football game at Wrigley Field on Sunday, Nov. 5. The boys were Tom and Mike Dolan, Norm Chilton, Bob Haggerty, Phil Kelsey, John Scott, Dick Cuthbertson, Jerry Engelbrecht and Dave McCullough. Coaches Marion Fox and Milt Truesdale were in charge of the group. After the game they all went to Research Hospital to visit Dave.

Bob Haggerty planned the many trips that he, Jack Walsh, Tom Dolan, Norm Chilton and Bob Diehl took to Research Hospital. At least once a month they took the train on Saturdays from Rockford, visited Dave and then stayed all night with Bob's uncle and aunt, Frank and Marge Cirrincione, in suburban River Forest.

Jack said they were scared of going to such a big city, scared of missing the train, scared of getting off at the wrong station and still scared of getting polio by going into the hospital.

But they went anyway.

On one visit, Dave asked them if they had brought him a beer. Not today, they replied. But on the next trip they smuggled in a beer, obtained for them by one of the older guys in Durand. Once the nurses left the room, they emptied a glass of water and poured in the beer. Dave sipped it through a straw.

Back in Rockford at St. Anthony's, Ed suffered a setback in mid-November when he developed respiratory acidosis, the increase of acidity in the blood and other body tissue. It was treated with fluids and blood transfusions. He recovered rapidly as his breathing, swallowing and use of his hands improved.

As Ed's condition improved, he was removed from his iron lung for two weeks. Unfortunately, he then developed breathing difficulties and had to be put back into the iron lung.

In Durand a week later, the high school basketball team opened its season against Byron, losing 55-51. Norm Chilton led Durand with 22 points.

Tom Dolan and Dave McCullough pretended they were play-by-play radio announcers and used the high school's tape recorder to tape all the home basketball games. The McCullough twins then visited Ed in Rockford and played the game tapes for him. Someone — Tom couldn't recall who but most likely it was Dave McCullough — took the bulky recording machine and tapes to Chicago and played them for Dave.

On Thanksgiving eve, Nov. 23, our family celebrated Joan's election to Homecoming Court. Barely a month out of the hospital, she — along with Bob Haggerty — was named second attendant on the Homecoming Court. The king was Phil Kelsey and the queen was Bev Meier. First attendants were Anita Bliss and Tom Dolan. The

Homecoming dance followed the basketball game with Pecatonica, which Durand won 45-42.

But the biggest news of the day was the homecoming of Rose after spending nearly three months in Township and St. Anthony's hospital.

The moment was captured by reporter Roger Hedges of *The Rockford Morning Star.*

"God sure must be taking good care of us or we wouldn't be so lucky," Dad told Hedges. "We have so much to be thankful for on Thanksgiving."

Mom spent much of the day preparing an 18-pound turkey and getting four of our sisters ready for the Homecoming dance. At the center of all the festivities was Rose, looking pale but smiling. Her therapy would continue daily at home and twice a week at St. Anthony's.

As Thanksgiving Day arrived, all our brothers and sisters except Dave and Ed joined in the meal that included potatoes, gravy, sweet potatoes, dressing, salads, nut bread, cranberries and pumpkin pies, all made by the older girls.

Immediately after dinner, Mom and Dad left for St. Anthony's, taking a generous portion of turkey and all the trimmings for Ed, who the day before had stood next to his rocking bed—the first time he had been on his feet in two months.

From Rockford, Mom and Dad traveled to Chicago to visit Dave in Research Hospital.

He was well enough to have his feeding tube removed. "He's eating mashed potatoes, pudding, ice cream and all sorts of things now," Dad said. "Sometimes he eats half the food the boy in the next bed doesn't want...the thing that keeps him going is that he wants to hurry up and come home."

The fund to help our family had now reached $9,302.41. Mom wrote a postcard to everyone who had sent a letter with a donation. It read:

"Please accept our heartfelt thanks for your contribution for our children. The kindness which prompted this has done much to alleviate our burden. God Bless You!
"Mr. and Mrs. Keron Walsh"

Another letter from Mom and Dad appeared Thanksgiving Day in *The Durand Gazette*. It read:

"At this Thanksgiving time we want to publicly thank you, our friends and neighbors; Rev. Father Driscoll for his many, many visits to the hospitals and to our home, for his prayers, for the nationwide plea for praying; the members of St. Mary's church for their generous response to the appeal for prayers; Rev. B.J. Usher for his repeated request for prayers and the wonderful response from members of the Methodist church; the members of the Lutheran church for their prayers and donation; the nurses of this community who went into the contagion ward and nursed our children; the Farm School for their donation and offer of help; the stores and places of business who donated to us; the many, many, many who donated food, who canned fruit and vegetables and made jellies for us; the men who did our chores for so many days; the neighbors who combined our clover, the 60 men who picked our corn at the corn-picking bee sponsored by the American Legion, St. Anne's Sodality and neighbors who prepared and served the meal for the cornpickers; the New England Grange who sponsored the dance and donated the proceeds to the members of our family who were stricken; Art Johnson, who is in charge of the Walsh Polio Fund; the post office personnel and mail carrier who handled our mail so well; those who helped answer our mail; the telephone operators who were deluged with calls; the teachers and pupils of Durand Community District for their visits, letters, cards and gifts; the 4-H clubs' leaders and members; all who contributed to the Walsh

Polio Fund; the many others too numerous to mention who wrote cards and letters and sent donations to us. We can only whisper our thanks and pray that God's choicest blessings be showered upon you—the truly helpful, generous, sympathetic people of Durand.
"Keron and Anne Walsh and family."

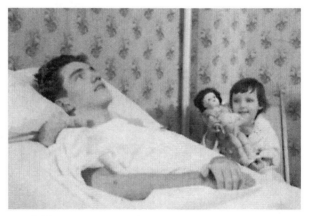

Less than two months after being released from St. Anthony's Hospital, where she was treated for polio, Joan, front left, joined the Homecoming Court in November 1955. With her are Beverly Meier, front center, Anita Bliss, front right, and standing, from left, Bob Haggerty, Phil Kelsey and Tom Dolan. (DHS yearbook).

Rose left her room at St. Anthony's with her doll Peggy to visit Ed in his room in November 1955. (Walsh family photo).

A closer look at Peggy and Rose. (Walsh family photo).

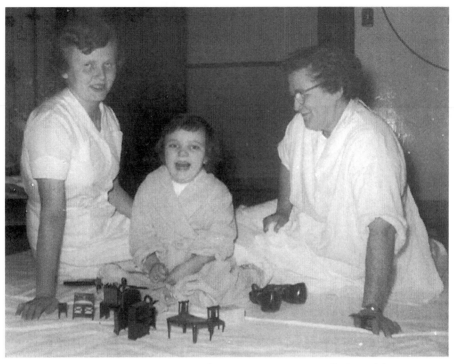

Rose, wearing the bathrobe she got from Roy Rogers and Dale Evans, with physical therapist Janet Cook, left, and an aide named Gussie. (Walsh family photo).

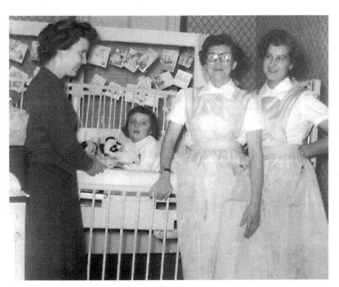

Lorraine, left, visits Rose at St. Anthony's, accompanied by two nurses' aides, Mary Jo Bartel and an unidentified aide, far right. (Walsh family photo).

92

CHAPTER 11:

A Reunion for Dave and Ed

Pictures of Black Angus cattle and Hampshire hogs on the walls confirmed that Dave continued to adjust in December to his new home in Room 1204 at Illinois Research Hospital.

He began planning his course of studies to earn a diploma in the spring at the same time his senior classmates would be graduating from Durand High School. A teacher from Spaulding High School in Chicago, Mrs. Margaret Dee, came twice a week to teach him civics and English. Another teacher in the hospital's orthopedic department, Mrs. Catherine Mahoney, also tutored Dave.

Occupational therapists showed Dave how to write with an electric typewriter, punching the keys with a stick held in his mouth. In high school Dave had been a struggling typist in teacher Roman Baker's class. Now Dave told visitors to tell Mr. Baker "I can type a heck of a lot better with a stick in my mouth than I ever did with two hands."

Dave also used the stick to turn pages when reading magazines placed in a rack above his head in his rocking bed. In addition, he mastered the art of reading books upside down. The books, like the magazines, were held in the special rack. He even learned how to itch his nose with his tongue. "He was willing to try anything," Alice said.

The rocking bed, used with a chest respirator, freed Dave from the conventional iron lung for up to five hours a day, according to Dr. Saxton, the hospital's director.

Father John W. Marren, pastor of Holy Trinity Catholic Church in

Chicago, brought Dave communion every Thursday.

"Dave's greatest quality is his consideration for others, especially for his family," Father Marren said. "He's more worried about his brother (Ed) than himself.

"He's pitching in to make the very best of a bad situation. It shows the good home and closely knit family he comes from."

With a tone of regret, Dave said he hadn't been able to decide on what Christmas gifts to give his family. All he expected was a letter from home.

"That's one of the best things," he said.

Letters were equally welcomed by Ed. One promising a puppy came in early December from Aunt Mary Mulcahy, Mom's sister.

"Your mother called last night and asked about a puppy. I just called Alice (Alice Carroll, Mom's cousin) and she said she has three little male puppies 8 or 9 weeks old which she will give to you — you can take your pick.

"One is long-haired, black and brown and some white. The other two are short-haired, sort of blackish-gray. The mother is a pure-bred Collie and the father is a sort of mongrel — he has short hair and looks as if he was part bird dog with a dash of (Airedale) thrown in.

"Have someone let us know which one you want and Alice said you can have them any time…maybe we could give it to your folks or leave it at Grandpa's or wherever or whenever you say."

Another letter, this one from Belgium, arrived but presented a challenge. "It's written in Flemish and there's no one around to interpret it," Dad said. "But I know just about what it says and I'm grateful that people so far away think of us and remember us in their prayers."

A Christmas newsletter issued by the Illinois Future Farmers of America called on all the state FFA chapters to contribute to a special fund established to assist Dave, the president of Durand's FFA chapter.

"I will admit there are many other people stricken with polio," wrote state vice president LeRoy Fischer in a letter to all state chapters.

"But I do not believe the cases are as serious as David's. Many of us read about the dreaded disease and forget about it, but I don't think we should forget David."

As Christmas neared, plans for the holiday were up in the air because many of us at home were suffering from an age-old illness — the common cold.

"We aren't sure we'll be able to do much of anything," Mom said. "We still have to be thankful for everything. We've got our Christmas tree up and we'll still open our gifts on Christmas Eve the way we always do."

Our Christmas celebration began with an oyster stew supper on Dec. 24. After supper we opened one or two gifts.

Christmas morning was busy at our house. The little ones were up early to see what Santa had left for them. This year it was Mom and Dad who were visited by Santa. His name was Ken Krienke. Mom saw him in the driveway while Dad was getting ready to go out to do the chores before attending Mass. Ken had left his own young family to do our early Christmas chores so that Dad would have more time with our family.

Earlier in the week, Dave received some Christmas cheer. Dad and our twin sisters Alice and Anne attended a Christmas party at Research Hospital for Dave and all the patients. They were moved into the hallways for a gift exchange and a visit from Santa Claus.

About the same time 25 of Ed's classmates visited him at St. Anthony's, set up a Christmas tree in his room, decorated it and held a Christmas party.

After the family gathering and celebration on Christmas morning at home and Mass at St. Mary's church, Dad, Mom, Joan and Sue left for Chicago to visit Dave. Alice and Anne went to Rockford to visit Ed.

A special Christmas gift was awaiting Ed. Dr. Leonard announced that he would be moved later in the week to Illinois Research Hospital to join Dave.

Ed was not being moved because of any worsening of his condition, Dr. Leonard said.

"It's going to be a hard pull for the boy, and I thought he and his brother should be together," the doctor added.

He said Ed was unable to be out of his iron lung more than an hour at a time, limiting the therapy he required. In Chicago, Ed would receive all the required therapy by using a chest respirator similar to the one Dave had used since sometime in November.

"Both boys are steadily improving and David looks much better in person than he does in newspaper pictures," Dr. Leonard said.

Moving day — Wednesday, Dec. 28, the birthdays of Joan and Julie (age 14) and Bill (11) — arrived for Ed. He was greeted for the send-off by about a dozen friends and relatives — Mom, Dad, Anne, Julie, Aunt Teresa, Father Driscoll, Uncle Joe Kenucane (Mom's brother), Luther McCullough and his twin sons Dan and Dave (Ed's classmates), classmate Dick Barron and Clarence Kleckner of the Infantile Paralysis Foundation.

Hospital attendants and nuns at St. Anthony's appeared to be saddened by Ed's leaving.

Ed, like Dave weeks earlier, was placed in an ambulance and hooked up to a special portable lung for the trip to Chicago. Aunt Teresa accompanied two other attendants in the ambulance. Dad, Mom, Anne and Julie followed in their own car.

As soon as they arrived at the hospital, Ed and his portable lung were wheeled into Dave's room.

"They were obviously happy" seeing one another, said Dr. Wolter. "But you know how teen-agers are. They never really say anything."

Our brothers were together for about 1½ hours before Ed was removed from the overcrowded room. Dave shared his room with a new, 17-year-old roommate, Dick Wolf, who also was using a rocking bed.

Dr. Wolter said Dave and Ed would become roommates as soon

as Ed was able to shed his iron lung and breathe properly in a rocking bed.

"It's difficult to say just how long it will be," she said. "We'll try him out right away, but sometimes it takes patients a little while to make the switch."

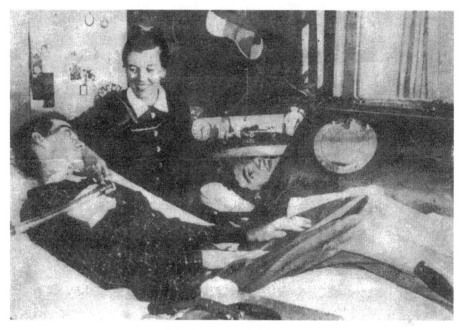

Aunt Teresa comforts Dave, left, and Ed after Ed was transferred in December 1955 to Illinois Research Hospital from St. Anthony's in Rockford. (United Press).

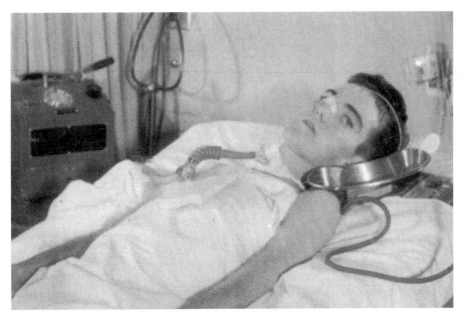

Dave resting at Illinois Research Hospital in Chicago. (Walsh family photo).

CHAPTER 12:

A New Crisis

New Year's Day 1956 began with *The Rockford Morning Star* saluting our family and declaring that our four-month ordeal with polio was one of the newspaper's "Stories of the Year."

Chicago's WLS radio station, and to a lesser degree WGN, began broadcasting daily updates on Dave and Ed's condition. On Jan. 4, Julie was listening to an early morning newscast on WGN when she was stunned to hear the broadcaster announce that Ed's body had taken on a greenish tint.

Worse yet, Ed fell into a coma and his left lung collapsed.

Doctors at Illinois Research Hospital said Ed's lung collapsed on Friday, Jan. 6, just hours after they had reported he had been making a slight improvement.

The collapsed lung cut Ed's air intake in half but the doctors compensated for the loss by increasing the pressure on oxygen being pumped into his right lung through a tube inserted in his tracheotomy.

"This sort of thing is fairly common with paralytic patients," said Dr. George A. Saxton, the director of the center. "The lung was so weak the walls stuck together and it just gave out."

He said Ed's condition had worsened since the unexpected setback and was listed as "critical."

While three hospital specialists worked round-the-clock shifts with Ed, researchers continued their search for the defect that turned his body green before he lapsed into a coma.

"This isn't a matter of pigment of the skin," a hospital spokesman said. "The serum in his blood has turned green. We know his body's green because of the blood but we haven't been able to determine what chemical process has affected the serum.

"Right before he became unconscious he was asking for more oxygen. But tests revealed he was getting the proper amount. No one can figure out why he isn't absorbing the necessary oxygen into his blood stream."

However, Dr. Saxton said the researchers had made discoveries that were bringing them closer to a solution.

Our family physician, Dr. Leonard, was called in for consultation. He said Ed's body had been taking on a greenish hue since late October while he was being treated at St. Anthony's Hospital in Rockford. Dr. Leonard also said he hoped that Illinois Research Hospital's specialized staff could solve the mystery of the coloring, believed to be the first case of a polio victim's body turning green.

In addition, Dr. Leonard said Ed had suffered several convulsions, "indicating a brain involvement of some kind." Ed's entire left side was badly weakened by the polio, the doctor said. He added that Dave was "looking better but he's crying all over the place" because of his brother's ordeal.

By Monday, Jan. 9, Ed's condition, still listed as "critical," slightly improved. His weakened left lung began showing some signs of re-inflation.

"There's a little air in the lung now, but it's so little they can't measure it," a hospital spokesman said.

In addition, hospital officials reported that Ed was actually in a semi-conscious condition, not in a full coma.

"He's able to do some grunting and groaning and shake his head in response to talking, although he still isn't able to speak," an official said.

Mom and Dad maintained a bedside vigil throughout Ed's treatment and were joined over the weekend by Aunt Teresa Houghton.

On Wednesday, Jan 11, Ed's lung filled with air and returned to normal after a small quantity of fluid was removed. But his condition remained "critical" and he was still in a semi-conscious state.

Mom's vigil at Ed's bedside was interrupted on Jan. 21 when she was named Winnebago County Polio Mother of the Year by the county chapter of the National Foundation of Infantile Paralysis and the 1956 March of Dimes.

From Chicago, Mom declared:

"It certainly is an honor to be named Polio Mother of the Year in Winnebago County. In the past few months I've found out how really horrible polio can be, and I pray no other mother experiences what happened to our family.

"I think our family's situation points out what polio can do. It proves that no matter who you are or how old you are, there is no escaping the dreaded disease until it's wiped out."

Ed's condition stabilized but remained critical well into the next month, until Feb. 15, when he came out of his semi-coma and was placed on the "fair condition" list.

A hospital official said Ed was "conscious, talking, recognizing things and remembering people." He was able to eat soft foods instead of being fed through a tube.

"If there is just a little improvement each month in a serious polio case like this," one of the doctors said, "we consider it a good accomplishment. Treating a case like this is a long process."

The official also said Ed's body no longer had a greenish tint. Doctors determined Ed's blood had turned green because of an oxygen deficiency but never could discover the underlying cause.

Alice recalls Mom using the term "cardiac collapse" when telling her about Ed's January setback. "Mother told me more than once she had to make a big decision in a hurry regarding Ed's emergency medical care when the hospital called one night to say he had had a cardiac collapse. Doctors needed to inject a drug directly into his heart.

Mom gave her permission but often wondered afterward if it was the right decision."

During Ed's ordeal, Dave continued his recovery. He was able to sit in a wheelchair about an hour a day. He enjoyed reading books and continued to operate an electric typewriter, using a mouth stick to press the keys. Attendants said he was in "very good spirits."

Dave's first letter written on the typewriter on Jan. 26 was to Mom. It said:

> *"Dear Ma,*
> *"Did you get home OK last night? We are alright here."*
> *"Dave"*

Aunt Teresa added her own note on the letter.

"What do you think of this for the second day on the typewriter?"

Except for a few days, Mom maintained her bedside vigil throughout Ed's crisis that began Jan. 4. She was accompanied at various times by Dad, Aunt Teresa, Aunt Margaret, Aunt Nita and some of our sisters.

The ordeal took its toll on Mom. Once she left the hospital briefly to cash a check. "But they wouldn't cash her check," cousin Mary Lou said. "Her I.D. showed a woman with black hair. Her hair was now white. It was the first time she noticed her hair had turned white."

CHAPTER 13:

A Special Graduation

Sunday, March 4 arrived and Dave celebrated his 18th birthday much as he would have if he was home on the farm.

The party at Illinois Research Hospital was arranged by Mom and Dad and a group of Dave's high school classmates. Dave had four birthday cakes: one baked by Mom, with enough for all 12 patients in the polio ward, and three brought by his classmates, who also came with candy, brownies and gifts.

Also attending were our sisters Alice and Julie and brothers Bernie and Tom. "It's kind of hard to decide just who we should take with us," Mom told a reporter. "The doctor says the boys should see their brothers and sisters but there are so many, and it's so crowded there, we can't take them all at once."

Ed, still very weak after his ordeal, wasn't able to join the celebration in Dave's room but shared in the visit of his family and schoolmates. School friends attending the party were Anita Bliss, Bev Meier, Sandra Bliss, Kathy and Phil Kelsey, Dan and Dave McCullough, Jerry Engelbrecht, Marilee Keller, Jane Walsh, Joyce Wise and Ken Waller.

Family members and school friends continued to visit Dave and Ed in Chicago though not as often as when the boys were in Rockford hospitals. An exception was Roger Sarver, Lorraine's classmate and the star guard on the 1953-54 basketball team that posted a 20-7 record, Durand's best ever at the time. Roger was attending a radio and television repair school in Chicago and during the week lived only about a half-mile from Illinois Research Hospital.

For several weeks, Roger walked almost daily to the hospital to see Dave and Ed. They often asked him to move their arms to a different position or to scratch a bothersome itch. He said sometimes they were next to each other in the same room and other times they were in different rooms. They were always upbeat, Roger added.

Once during a visit when Mom and Dad also were there, a nurse opened the iron lung to do something for Ed. Roger wanted to leave the room because Ed wasn't breathing when the iron lung was open. Dad told him to stay. The nurse closed the iron lung and Ed started breathing again. It was almost too much to watch, Roger said.

Another school friend, Carole Cowan, lived in Chicago when she was attending the Patricia Stevens School of Modeling and occasionally visited Dave and Ed. She often read newspaper articles to Dave. She said she did not have as much contact with Ed because his condition and voice were much weaker than Dave's.

Another occasional visitor was Sandy Berg, a high school student whose mother Marion Berg was one of the nurses caring for Dave and Ed while they were in Rockford Township Hospital. Sandy visited the boys both in Rockford and Chicago, usually with her parents. When she discovered that Dave liked car racing, she reported to both of the boys the previous week's race results at the Rockford Speedway.

"I loved going to visit them," Sandy said. "They would have me laughing. How they could be so jolly, I just couldn't figure it out. All I can say is that they brightened my day."

Another regular visitor in Chicago was a priest, Father Mark Hoban, from the Marmion Military Academy, a Catholic high school for boys in suburban Aurora. Mom and he became good friends and remained so for the next several years.

Our family members often took the train to visit Dave and Ed in Chicago. Our sister Anne remembers seeing row after row of iron lungs in the polio ward, many containing young people and even some expectant mothers.

Relatives and school friends continued to write letters to Dave and Ed but none wrote more often than Anne. For months she wrote Dave nearly every day, so often that she ran out of envelopes and was forced to mail three or four letters in a single envelope until she bought new ones.

She kept Dave informed of the daily routine at school and home.

"It is really snowing right now. I think there was an inch of ice on the tank this morning when we did the chores...

"I just ordered your graduation announcements. I got 18 and 100 name cards. I think that ought to be enough. The honor roll is on the board right now...Alice, Karen Holland and John Dickerson all got straight A's...We had two new calves the last two nights. I think we have about 20 calves. The new bull is so cute...

"The juniors got Ed's class ring today and they are going to give it to one of us to bring it home...Last night Bob Walsh, Ken Krienke, Bill and Don Stockdale and Dwight Boomer came out to do the chores...That picture that was in the *Sun-Times* of you and Ed was in the San Diego, California, paper also...

"Today the seniors had to write poetry in class. Bob Haggerty wrote a terrible poem and Mrs. Johnson got ahold of it and kept him after class. I would have hated to be him. Wow!

"Dad, Jerry (Engelbrecht) and Bill went over south and some of the trees were just covered with seventeen year locusts. They brought some home and Bill is having a picnic scaring the little girls...

"Molly is just full of HELL! We can't do a thing with her. She is getting cuter as the days go by...I just found out Molly is going to sleep with me. Oh Brother! That means no sleep tonight."

Anne nearly always signed her letters, "Love and Prayers."

In early April, all of our hopes were raised when we learned that a motorized wheelchair was being built for Dave to use if he was able to return home.

A hospital spokesman said doctors hoped to have both Dave and Ed return home sometime in the summer.

"However," he said, "I emphasize we use the word hope and that's all we can do."

Mrs. Doris McMillin, executive secretary of the Winnebago County chapter of the National Foundation for Infantile Paralysis, said she was asked by Dr. Saxton to provide the wheelchair.

The specially designed chair was being built in the hospital's workshop. The project was financed with $450 from the fund established for our family. Mrs. McMillin added that the fund would continue to pay all our polio expenses until it was exhausted. At that point, she said the polio foundation would pick up the costs.

The wheelchair would be equipped with an electric motor and rigged so Dave could operate it by using only his head. Both boys used a wheelchair on occasion but Ed was still bedfast most of the time. The plan was that neither would be able to leave the hospital until they regained their ability to breathe unassisted. Both still had oxygen pumped through small tubes in their windpipes.

Dave was measured for a fitted plastic chest respirator, which would operate by air pressure to help his lungs and diaphragm function properly while he regained his ability to breathe.

Both boys were getting along "very well" and Ed's condition was the best it had been since he fell into a coma and his lung collapsed in early January, Dr. Saxton said in April. He added that Dave had developed several kidney stones and attendants were considering removing them.

A few days later, Dr. Saxton changed his mind about Dave and Ed needing to be able to breathe unassisted before returning home. The doctor called Mom into his office and shocked her with his news.

"He said they were sending our boys home for us to care for them," Mom said.

"I was terrified.

"I was not a nurse and our closest doctor was over 20 miles away.

But Dr. Saxton said, 'You know, now, more than most doctors know about polio.'

"Their life depended on respirators and rocking beds. He was serious since they were beyond help.

"So we took our money, saved for later days, and began building a room where the boys would stay."

Back on the farm, where spring was a busy time, Dad gave up his membership on the board of the Winnebago County Farm Bureau. His daily chores and constant trips to Chicago to visit Dave and Ed left little time for board work.

Helping out with the chores now was our new hired hand, Jerry Engelbrecht, a neighbor and Ed's classmate. Also pitching in was 15-year-old Anne, feeding the pigs and carrying the silage before school. Bill, now 11 and the oldest boy on the farm, helped with the chores and milked one or two cows, despite hating "pigs and chickens and doing chores…All I want to do is plow and ride my pony."

Lorraine also helped in the fields, driving a tractor and helping Dad disc and drag in preparing the fields for planting oats.

Dave and Ed continued to be tutored, with Dave concentrating on earning enough credits to receive his diploma with his class. His studies included general education classes and special agricultural classes.

On May 29, Dave's classmates received their diplomas at a graduation ceremony at Durand High School. Most of his classmates then prepared to attend the special graduation exercises for Dave on Sunday, June 3, at Illinois Research Hospital.

Supt. Paul G. Norsworthy presided at the ceremony, attended by more than 100 people, mostly from Durand and including several of our relatives and many on the hospital staff.

Ed, still weak after his January crisis, attended part of the ceremony. Both he and Dave were in wheelchairs and were attached to portable respirators.

The ceremony brought Mom and Dad and all of us 14 children

together for the first time since polio struck last September.

Father Driscoll gave the commencement address. He likened the courage of Dave to that of King David of the Bible and said those attending the ceremony should feel "that they were honored to be present with David, rather than to honor him."

Carlyle Horstmeier played the processional music, "Pomp and Circumstance," as Dave was wheeled into the hospital auditorium wearing his blue-and-white cap and gown and followed by 17 of his 23 classmates wearing their caps and gowns.

Supt. Norsworthy then presented Dave his diploma.

The Chicago Tribune captured the scene.

"With both smiles and tears, David's parents glanced alternately in three directions. First they would look at their son on the stage. Then their eyes would turn to their second son, Edward, 16, sitting in a wheelchair and using a respirator. Finally they would look to the front row where 12 of their other children were sitting. Among them was Rose Ellen, 5, restlessly adjusting a corset brace she must wear because of the disease.

"Like most other graduating seniors David was excited. 'O boy, the day is finally here,' he told his classmates, who voted him graduate of the year and gave him $50 from the class fund. He also was presented with an autograph book, signed by all members of his class, and a class picture."

The graduation program included a reception afterward arranged by our family and members of the hospital staff, who had taken our brothers into their hearts. Our twin sisters, Anne and Alice and Joan and Julie, presided at the reception featuring punch and a large cake. When the affair was over, the cake was taken to Dave's ward, where a party was held for the patients there.

Attending the graduation were 17 of Dave's classmates: Norm Chilton, Sylvia Clark, Bob Diehl, Tom Dolan, Mary Englebrecht, Beverly Fosler, Gloria Fox, Kay Guehring, Bob Haggerty, Carlyle Horstmeier,

Jane Larson, Sally Stettler, Dan Waller (class president), Don Waller, Jack Walsh, Phyllis Weires and Carol Whisman.

A little fatigued from the excitement, Dave still smiled as he was wheeled back into his room and the visitors left for home. "It sure feels great to have this diploma," he said.

The next week, *The Durand Gazette* published a letter from "A Citizen" who saluted the town and celebrated Dave's graduation:

"Durand might not be a large town as large towns are reckoned, but I defy anyone to find a town with a heart as large, a heart as sympathetic, a heart as full of true Christian love!

"On Sunday, June 3, we saw a wonderful example of the kind of people who live here. A busy school superintendent took the time and made the effort to make arrangements for the high school graduating class of 1956 to go to Chicago so that a brave 18-year-old boy hospitalized with polio might be part of the graduating class. A busy pastor, after having celebrated two Masses and tended to the spiritual needs of both of his parishes, made the trip to speak words of encouragement and benediction for this lad. Many parents of the graduating classmates whose hearts reached out in understanding of what it meant to a fun-loving boy to be surrounded by his friends and classmates took their children the 100 miles to be present at the graduation. Loving relatives and friends arranged for refreshments so that it might be a gala affair for David.

"Time and again during the past months since polio struck the Walsh family, there have been countless examples of Durand's open and loving heart, but never more clearly than on Sunday.

"As Durand prepares to celebrate its Centennial year, it might appear that she has made little progress, but in what large city would one find the love and understanding of human needs so freely demonstrated? From now on, I shall proudly square my shoulders and announce: 'Yes, I'm from Durand, the little town whose people have hearts of gold."

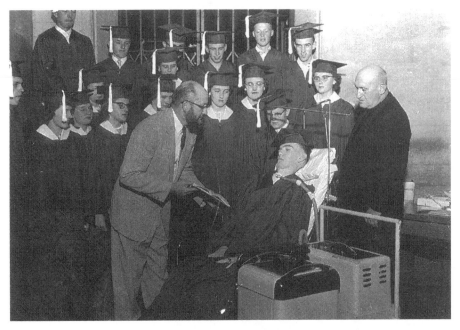

Dave is awarded his diploma by Supt. Paul G. Norsworthy, center, as 17 of his senior classmates watch the ceremony on June 3, 1956 at Illinois Research Hospital. At top right are Tom Dolan, Norm Chilton and Jack Walsh. Father Driscoll is standing behind Dave. In the foreground are Dave's portable respirators. (Walsh family photo).

Dave with five of his classmates at the graduation ceremony. From left are Tom Dolan, Carlyle Horstmeier, Jack Walsh, Norm Chilton and Bob Haggerty. (Walsh family photo).

CHAPTER 14:

Celebrating Durand's Centennial

T*he Durand Gazette*'s anonymous letter writer was especially timely in mentioning the upcoming Centennial — the big celebration would begin in about six weeks. Lorraine was a candidate to be queen of the Centennial and plans were well underway for Dave to attend, if only for a weekend. But Dave couldn't come home until the special room for him and Ed was added to our house.

After Dr. Saxton's decision in April to send the boys home sometime in the summer, Dad immediately hired Evans Whitman to build the additional room on the front of our house.

Whitman was considered by many in Durand to be the best carpenter in the area. A few years earlier Dad had hired him to add two bedrooms and a bath on the second floor, build our garage and, in 1949, our new barn.

To celebrate completion of the barn, Dad held a huge barn dance in the new haymow on Saturday, Oct. 8, 1949. The dance featured a popular five-member band, Captain Stubby and the Buccaneers, stars of a regular program on WLS radio in Chicago. Hundreds of area folks attended the barn dance, where Lorraine, then 12, first danced with a boy. The dance was so successful that Dad held a second one on Sunday, Oct. 16, this time featuring the Bill Hartwig Band from Wisconsin.

Now, seven years later, Whitman and his crew — it was composed of several area men including Bill Flynn and Jon Dixon, a member of the great 1953-54 Durand basketball team — focused on building the new room designed by Dad and Mom. Plans called for it to be large enough for two rocking beds, a large elevated tub for bathing, mechanical lifts, respirators, suction equipment and a small bathroom.

The final size was 20 feet by 24 feet with large windows on three sides. This would allow the boys to watch the activity outside on the farm, such as when the cattle were moved from lot to field, or when tractors came and went or when bales of hay were put on the elevator to the haymow. A generator would be installed in our basement to keep the rocking beds operating in case of a power failure.

During the construction, Bill, Bernie and Tom decided to play a practical joke on Fran, then age 4. She loved her red blanket that she slept with and carried nearly everywhere she went. The boys hid it under the floor of the new room. The minute Fran missed it, "she raised such a ruckus that the carpenters had to tear up a piece of the floor to try to retrieve it," Bernie said. They never did find it.

"It was gone forever, my 'blanky,' red and so soft," Fran recalled years later. "Mom did buy me a new outfit, a navy and white dress with a coat to match, for being brave." And 20 years later, Rose made Fran a new red blanket.

When the room was finished days before the Centennial celebration began, "it looked absolutely beautiful with knotty pine walls, tiled floor and very large windows," Julie said. A social worker and other officials from Illinois Research Hospital inspected it and "were very pleased with everything," Julie added. "So we began making arrangements for around-the-clock nursing care."

Dave continued to write notes on his typewriter using a mouth stick to punch the keys. On Friday, June 15, he typed a special Father's Day note to Dad.

Despite Dave's comments, Ed was not "feeling pretty good." He continued to be in a weakened condition so a weekend pass for the Centennial for him was out of the question. Still, he experienced his own celebrations. Several classmates visited him in early July in advance of his 17th birthday. Making the trip from Durand for the birthday party were Anita Bliss, Kathy Kelsey, Joyce Wise, Jane Walsh, Dan and Dave McCullough, Jerry Engelbrecht and Phil Kelsey. And Mom was with Ed on his actual birthdate, July 13.

All of us also were excited by Lorraine's entry into the contest to be queen of the Centennial. The winner would be the contestant who had the most tickets sold in her

```
                              June 15, 1956
Dear Dad,

        Happy Fathers Day to you.
The card we had for you got lost
so this one will have todo.

        How is everyone at home getting
alohe? Ed and I feeling pretty'
good.

        Aße you getting along hay-
ing ok? Was the weather been
alful hot the last week out there?
IT has been in upper 90's al-
most every day in here. How is
the corn standing the weather,
it proably needs rain pretty
bad doesn't it?

        Are Joe and florence and Dick
Shitley coming in Sunday?

        I have to close now, be see-
ing you.              Your sons,
                      Dave andEd
```

Dave's Father's Day note to Dad in June 1956. Dave used a mouth stick to punch the typewriter keys.

name to the Centennial pageant. Buyers voted for queen by purchasing tickets from them.

After a slow start, Lorraine "vaulted from fourth place to first place and now leads all contestants in the battle for the Durand Centennial queen title," *The Rockford Morning Star* reported on Sunday, July 8.

"Exact vote totals (of ticket sales) are not available, so the margin between Lorraine and her nearest rival, June Raddatz, is not available. The winner will be revealed Wednesday night at the Queen's Ball at the grade school gymnasium and crowned Thursday by Illinois Gov. William Stratton."

Ward Waller, the president of the Centennial, presided at the Queen's Ball. He had been in the job only three months after replacing Lloyd Mulvain, the star shortstop on the Durand Merchants outstanding softball team and a power company lineman who was electrocuted in a farmhouse accident in Shirland.

To the fanfare of music by Dulse Liston's 10-piece band, Waller made the announcement that the crowd of more than 700 attending the dance was waiting for — Lorraine Walsh was the winner and the Queen of the Centennial. The other six finalists were June Raddatz, Sandra Bliss, Betty Keller, Pat Smith, Sandra Tallakson and Delores Davis.

The next afternoon, in the Centennial's official opening ceremony in Town Square Park under the stately shady elm trees, Gov. Stratton crowned Lorraine in front of more than 1,000 people.

The Rockford Morning Star captured the moment.

"Miss Walsh, the girl who 'kept the home fires burning' last year while her parents cared for 10 brothers and sisters suffering from polio and later forsook a college career, had the diamond crown placed on her head as she stood resplendent in the regal robes of her Centennial post.

"Gov. Stratton also crowned Sally Langley, 7, Centennial princess, and Bernard Walsh, 8-year-old brother of Lorraine, as prince of the four-day celebration.

"He then praised Durand and its residents and told the crowd it was a pleasure to be on hand to join with them to crown a queen 'so lovely it took a hundred years to produce her.'

"'Durand didn't just happen,' the governor said. 'People gave of themselves down through history so that communities like this would flourish and live.'"

After the ceremony, our sister Molly, then 2 ½ years old, was not the least bit impressed at being held by the governor. When he took Molly in his arms, she immediately began crying and clutching for the more familiar arms of Mom.

Among more than a dozen dignitaries attending the ceremony were State's Attorney Robert R. Canfield, state Rep. Merle K. Anderson, County Republican Chairman H. Emmett Folgate, County Clerk

Horace M. Skinner, County Supt. of Schools Paul S. Conklin, attorney John B. Anderson and Durand Mayor Ernest Baker.

Lorraine wasn't our only sister reaping a Centennial award. That evening at the opening of the pageant at Legion Memorial Field, our sister Alice and Dan Waller were named Outstanding Young Citizens of Durand and presented with $25 savings bonds.

Alice and Anne played Indian maidens and Joan, Julie and Sue also were members of the cast of more than 200 in the pageant, entitled "Days of Durand." The cast acted out in pantomime 14 episodes dealing with the history of Durand as four narrators provided the spoken words. Tom and Mike Dolan were also cast members, playing Confederate Army soldiers. The pageant drew more than 5,500 in four nights.

Years later, Lorraine said she was "certain I was Centennial queen because of our family's ordeal. Marian Walsh sold many, many tickets for me — she took them to work and also worked hard around Durand selling them. The prize for the queen was a trip to New York City. She could take one person with her so I took Marian. We had an interesting tour of the city."

On Saturday, July 14, in Chicago, Dave was awarded his weekend pass and placed in Dad's new green Ford station wagon for a trip to Durand to see the Centennial parade. Dad and Uncle Leonard were in the front seats and Aunt Teresa Houghton and nurse Marion Berg accompanied Dave in the back seats. He wore a chest respirator and a suction device attached to his mouth to help him swallow.

A huge crowd of more than 15,000 jammed the town for the parade, which featured 135 units and took well over an hour to pass the reviewing stand.

"Dave was to be in Aunt Margaret and Uncle Leonard's front yard on Howard Street," Lorraine said. "I was riding in a convertible when the parade went by the house but Dave wasn't there.

"As soon as I could, I got in the car and went home. Dave had trouble breathing coming out from Chicago so they went straight to our house and placed him on the rocking bed."

When Julie saw Dave for the first time in his rocking bed, "I was shocked at how he looked.

"There was my big brother on the rocking bed which was going steadily up and down like a teeter totter. He was very pale, exceedingly thin with no evidence of any muscles at all, just skin and bones.

"He looked like people in photos of starving prisoners during the Holocaust. He could turn his head from side to side but was unable to move his arms or legs. His arms were positioned across his chest where they remained until he asked for someone to move them now and then."

Dave stayed home as planned until Monday, when he was taken back to Illinois Research Hospital, still hoping to return home in the near future.

A couple of weeks after the Centennial celebration, *The Durand Gazette* published a letter from Lorraine. It read:

"I would like to take the opportunity once again to thank the many wonderful people who made it possible, in any way, for me to reign as Queen of the Durand Centennial. It, indeed, was one of the greatest thrills of my life and I will cherish the honor the rest of my life.

"Our trip to New York City was tops. We were flown to New York by American Airlines and our accommodations were at the Waldorf Astoria. The tour included Lower Manhattan, Chinatown, Upper Manhattan, Statue of Liberty, Empire State Building, St. Patrick's Cathedral, The Bowery, a three-hour cruise around Manhattan, dinner at the Latin Quarter and a stage show, "No Time for Sergeants," in Times Square. Our return trip was on American Airlines also. I enjoyed every moment of it. Many, many thanks to

each and every one of you.
"Lorraine Walsh"

Meanwhile, banker Art Johnson announced that the entire $9,516 contributed to the fund set up to help our family had been spent. Most of the money, $7,587, was spent for hospital bills. Nurses' fees cost $1,312. The remainder went for doctors, ambulances, physical therapy, equipment and blood transfusions.

Clarence W. Kleckner, chairman of the Winnebago County chapter of the National Foundation for Infantile Paralysis, reported that the fund's money carried our family to May 1956. He said our family paid all the medical expenses in May and the polio chapter took over the expenses on June 1.

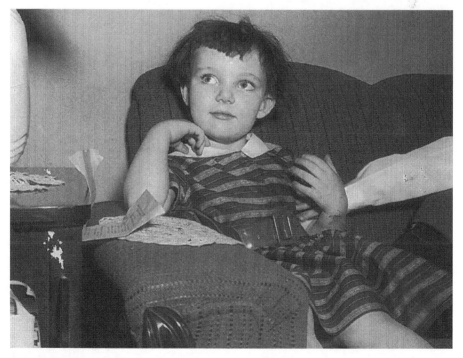

Rose on Grandpa and Grandma Kenucane's couch in Beloit sometime in 1956. (Walsh family photo).

Lorraine signs up in June 1956 for the Durand Centennial queen's contest.

Contestants for the Centennial contest, from left: Sandra Tallakson, Betty Keller, June Raddatz, Lorraine, Sandra Bliss, June Nelson and Pat Smith.

118

Above, Lorraine is stunned when she is announced as the winner of the queen's contest at the Queen's Ball on July 11, 1956.

Left, Lorraine is crowned as queen of the Centennial by Illinois Gov. William G. Stratton.

At left, Ward Waller, president of the Centennial, is sentenced at the Kangaroo Court to wheel Ken Krienke three times around Durand's Town Square Park.

John Walsh, Jack Walsh's dad, tends to business at St. Mary's snack shop during the Centennial.

Banker Art Johnson and a friend sing at Johnson's Kangaroo Court session.

Our cousin Bob Walsh.

Supt. Paul G. Norsworthy.

Mailman Floyd "Bump" Sarver.

Neighbor Bob Dobler.

Bev Meier, left, and Carole Cowan getting ready to model their playsuit and swimsuit in the Centennial fashion show. At right is Dan McCullough.

Dressed as Indian maidens for their roles in the Centennial Pageant are, from left: Sue Waller, Judy Smith and Anne and Alice.

Playing rebel soldiers in the pageant are, from left, Bob Smith, Dale Clark, Mike Dolan, Don Moore and Tom Dolan.

Ken Krienke portrays Abraham Lincoln in the pageant.

Mayor Ernest Baker escorts Queen Lorraine on the last night of the pageant.

A DAY FOR THE WALSHES—Governor and Mrs. William G. Stratton paused before Thursday's Durand centennial coronation ceremonies to visit with Keron and Ann Walsh, courageous Durand parents who last year guided the fortunes of their family as it was plagued with a serious polio epidemic. Shown in the photo above are, left to right, Governor Stratton; Mrs. Walsh, Winnebago county polio mother of the year; Mollie Walsh, 2½, in her mother's arms; Frances Walsh, 4; Keron Walsh; Rose Ellen Walsh, 5; and Mrs. Stratton. (Morning Star Photos by Fred F. James. Additional photos and story on front page.)

All the uncredited Durand Centennial photographs were taken by Dave McCullough and Dick Barron and are courtesy of Mo Ostergard and Dennis Bliss.

CHAPTER 15:

Broken Hearts

Two weeks after the Centennial, Dave received a letter from Durand School Supt. Paul G. Norsworthy, who was responding to Dave's thank-you note for arranging his graduation ceremony.

"I'm afraid you are giving me too much credit for that," the superintendent wrote. "Your teacher there at the hospital, the public relations division of the hospital, Dan Waller and a lot of other people did all the work and I should not accept credit for it.

"Tell Ed that it is less than a month until school starts again and that he had better be getting in shape for his studies.

"The noon whistle just blew and chow is waiting for me. I am going to play truant this afternoon and work on the new garage we are building."

But Ed was not in any condition to be "getting in shape for his studies." As Anne described it, "poor little Eddie started slowly going downhill. He contracted something the doctors referred to as looking like purple grapes in his lung."

Julie was downstairs at home early on the morning of Aug. 21. Mom was already dressed, planning to get an early start to Chicago to visit Dave and Ed. As she was about to leave, the phone rang. Mom answered it and listened briefly before crying out, "Why didn't you call me? Why didn't you call?" She told the doctor on the other end of the line that she and Dad would be there as soon as possible. She hung up and told us the horrible news.

Ed had died.

The news was devastating and unbelievable for all of us.

"I had never felt so sad," Julie said.

The boy who just a year earlier was so strong that even bigger boys couldn't beat him at arm wrestling, who in the flick of a second could answer nearly every trivia-type question ever put to him, who had built so many things around our farm including the shadow box for our Christmas nativity scene, who loved helping his classmates with their algebra, died early in the morning of Aug. 21 after having an emergency tracheotomy.

Though Dave was present, Ed, in effect, died alone.

Dave was in his iron lung next to Ed but could do nothing for him, "not even raise a finger to wipe away his own tears," Mom said.

The fact that Mom and Dad were not with Ed only added to our grief.

So now instead of arranging for Ed's transfer home to his new room, Mom and Dad began planning for his funeral. But first, Bernice Carroll drove them to Illinois Research Hospital so they could make arrangements there and be with Dave. They then decided that since Ed never was able to come home, they would have his body brought home for the wake.

All of our grief weighed heavy but Bernie's was worse, tainted by guilt.

Just a few months earlier, he had visited Dave and Ed in Chicago. Because Ed couldn't talk, Bernie spent most of the time that day with Dave. "After Ed died, I felt bad for a long time because I didn't want to spend more time with Ed that day," Bernie said.

In fact, Ed rarely spoke after suffering his cardiac episode in January, so Bernie was not alone in spending little time with him.

The Rockford Register-Republic screamed out the news of Ed's death in a huge Page One headline above the paper's masthead in its afternoon edition on Aug. 21. The next morning's *Rockford Morning Star* also published a Page One story under a large two-column headline. The articles reported that Ed died at 7:10 a.m. but the death certificate filed the same day said the time of death was 5:50 a.m. A hospital spokesman said doctors performed the emergency tracheotomy when Ed did not respond satisfactorily to respiratory treatment.

The death certificate said the immediate cause of death was "respiratory failure" and listed the underlying causes as "aspiration pneumonitis and pulmonary edema, bilateral, due to poliomyelitis (late effect)."

The planning and work for the wake and funeral began immediately. Father Driscoll and funeral director Floy Chapin were consulted. The wake would be at our home Thursday evening, Aug. 23, and the funeral would be Friday morning at St. Mary's.

Our older sisters, relatives and women from St. Mary's descended on our house to perform a "super cleaning" that included washing walls, taking down and cleaning every light fixture and waxing all the tile floors.

"Everyone seemed to have a bucket," Sue said. "Mom was horrified to let anyone see how much the house needed to be cleaned."

"We cleaned through our tears," Julie said.

"I'll never forget when my dear, gentle, precious Aunt Mary came to me, put her arm around me and said, 'Julia, I know how you feel. I was very sad, too, when my brother Tom died.' I wanted to yell out, 'no, no, you don't know how I feel because no one has ever felt this sad.' But I said nothing because I knew she was sad, too, and I did not want to make things worse for her."

After the cleaning, many of the helpers brought in chairs and set them up around the edges of the living room, dining room and into the new room addition. Beautiful flower arrangements were delivered Wednesday and Thursday.

On the afternoon of the wake, the hearse from Chapin's Funeral Home drove in to the driveway and parked.

"We watched as men from the funeral home brought Ed home in his casket," Julie said. "The flower bouquets were arranged around the casket, which was open for viewing.

"All of us were in a state of shock and deep, deep grief. We cried and hugged and cried some more. We knelt and said the rosary and other prayers for Ed."

The house was especially quiet for a few hours, Lorraine recalled, before people began arriving later that afternoon for the wake and rosary. The house filled up quickly and lines of mourners waited outside for their turn to say a final goodbye to Ed and to comfort Mom and Dad and all of us.

Bill served as the Doorman. He thought the line would never end. Cars were parked all the way up the hill on both sides of Baker Road.

In the early evening, Father Driscoll led the praying of the rosary. The crowd gradually dwindled but a few close relatives stayed until late into the night.

The next morning, the casket was loaded into Chapin's hearse and began its slow journey to Durand and St. Mary's. The church bells tolled for the longest time and a constant stream of cars passed the house of Coach Sid and Betty Felder's house on West Main Street on the way up the hill to St. Mary's. "It was very touching and sad," Betty Felder said.

Very few people remember any details of the funeral mass. Tom and Mike Dolan, Bob Haggerty and Dan Waller served as the altar boys and Dave and Dan McCullough served as pall bearers. But none of the dozens of people interviewed years later or anyone in our family can recall the names of the other pall bearers. Most likely they included Tom Spelman, Jerry Engelbrecht and Phil Kelsey.

Bev Waller said that she and several of Ed's classmates sat in the fourth row from the back of the church on the west side of the aisle.

"I don't remember many details except that the church was overflowing and Father Driscoll felt so sad while saying the Mass," Julie said.

"Going to the cemetery was dreadful but leaving it was even worse. My brother Ed was left there, his grave under a beautiful maple tree in the quiet of the country cemetery."

After the funeral and burial, we all returned to our house for a meal. The house again was filled with people helping themselves to food brought by many friends. Our sisters helped serve the tables that had been set up in every available space. Women from St. Mary's also helped serve the meal.

One of them, Jack Walsh's mother, Helen, served the priests at the head table. She asked them if they wanted ice cream or cheese served with apple pie. Cheese, one of the priests said. "That's good because apple pie without cheese is like a kiss without a squeeze," Helen replied. Everyone laughed, except some of our aunts, who wondered if the comment was appropriate to be said to a priest.

The next week, *The Durand Gazette* published a letter from Mom and Dad. It read:

> *"We wish to express our thanks to the many people who helped us in so many ways at the time of the sickness and death of our dear son, Edward.*
> *"Mr. and Mrs. Keron Walsh and family."*

At the same time, *The Beloit Daily News* saluted Ed and our family in an editorial. It read, in part:

"Edward, who would have been a senior in Durand High School this school year, made a courageous fight for life. He was a young man of promise.

"Despite the tragic circumstances that attended the Walsh family, the members have been steadfast in their faith and courage. They certainly stand in the minds of most of us as exemplary in the face of misfortune."

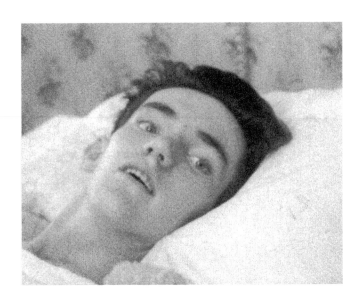

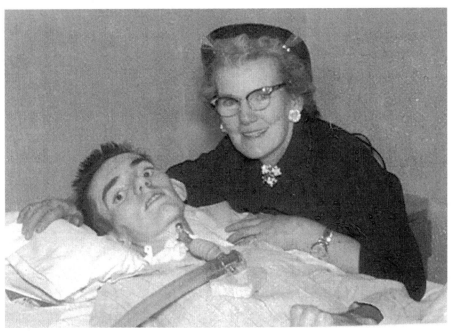

Mom visits Ed at Illinois Research Hospital on his 17th birthday on July 13, 1956.
(Walsh family photo).

CHAPTER 16:

Home at Last

After Ed's death, which left a huge void in Dave's life, officials at Illinois Research Hospital immediately began planning to transfer Dave to his new special room at our home. But a major snag blocked the path home: qualified practical nurses to care for him couldn't be found.

Dave was lonesome and homesick, said Doris McMillin, executive director of the Rockford chapter of the National Foundation for Infantile Paralysis. "Since Eddie died he wants to come home so badly," she said. "But it's been sort of a desperate battle for the last two months trying to find someone."

On Aug. 31, officials at St. Anthony's Hospital in Rockford announced that Dave would be transferred to St. Anthony's until some nurses were found. Dr. Leonard proposed the transfer to custodial care in Rockford while members of our family were taught how to care for him.

But a day later, the plan was scrapped.

"The people in Chicago said they want to hold him another week," Dr. Leonard said. "They've built him up for the trip home and they don't want to disappoint him by putting him in another hospital."

The wait finally ended.

Mrs. Carrie Fowler of Brodhead, Wis., and Mrs. Julie Hadie of Rockton, Ill. came forward and Illinois Research Hospital restored its plans for Dave's transfer home.

"We had all kinds of trouble finding nurses until these two women showed up," said a hospital spokesman in Chicago. "They both said they had been following the Walsh story in *The Morning Star* and when they learned nurses were needed they offered their services."

In all, about 30 nurses applied for the job after the story detailing the search for help appeared in the paper.

The two nurses spent two days at the Chicago hospital learning how to take care of Dave and his equipment. Special attention was given to the latest addition to his long list of mechanical aids — a motorized wheelchair.

By pressing his chin to an electromatic bar, Dave would be able to propel and steer the wheelchair at home.

Mrs. Fowler and Mrs. Hadie planned to work 9-hour shifts in our home, one from 8 a.m. to 5 p.m. and the other from 9 p.m. to 6 a.m.

On the eve of Dave's departure, Sept. 7, hospital officials were lavish in their praise of his courage and his cooperation, which they said made it possible for polio specialists to develop and perfect techniques that proved helpful to other patients.

"David's been doing as much as possible to take care of himself as long as he's been here," a hospital spokesman said. "As soon as he got here he moved from the iron lung to positive pressure devices that made it possible for therapists to work on him. And now he has learned 'frog breathing,' and that takes lots of courage."

The spokesman described "frog breathing" as a method by which the patient fills his lungs through a series of difficult gulps. By doing this, Dave was able to be free of mechanical aids periodically each day.

"David spends most of his time on a rocking bed now," the spokesman said. "And since a rocking bed is just about the least effective breathing aid there is, it indicates he's doing plenty of the work himself."

Mom and Dad drove to Chicago early Saturday morning, Sept. 8, to pick up Dave. Doctors placed Dave in the back of our family station wagon, where Mrs. Fowler tended the portable chest respirator Dave wore and also carried an emergency breathing apparatus to be used if the respirator failed.

Leaving the hospital was not easy.

Dave had "a couple of hard days" saying goodbye to everyone, Mrs. Fowler said. Dave said he made many friends while in Chicago and appreciated all the efforts made on his behalf.

He was all smiles when the family car pulled into a Rockford service station on the way home. When asked by a reporter how it felt to be going home, Dave replied, "Fine."

Throughout the trip, Dave constantly assured Mom and Dad that the portable respirator was working all right and that there was nothing to worry about.

Mom smiled when asked how it was to have Dave back home again. "It certainly will be good," she said. Dad beamed with pride and joy with the thought of having his oldest son home.

When Dave got home and was being pushed in his wheelchair up the ramp to his new room, he asked to stop so someone could place his hand on the grass.

Waiting at the farm were all of us—12 sisters and brothers—who quickly gathered around Dave's rocking bed once he was settled in and comfortable.

Dave was delighted to be home.

And we were delighted to have him home, although Julie said "it took a few days to feel comfortable around him but eventually I took turns with my sisters and others to stay in the room with him.

"He was so cheerful, so interested in everything we were doing, so precious as he asked us to scratch an itchy spot or move his hands or give him a drink of water.

"We fed him his meals while he rocked up and down. When the head of the bed came up, we would put the food in his mouth or give him a drink through a straw. We had to act quickly before the head of the bed started down again."

"Dave ate well," Alice said. "He loved Mother's homemade goulash. He was always interested in what was going on at school and on the farm. After being around both of the boys, I felt I had been close to God. After helping them I decided to be a nurse."

Sue recalled helping Mom help Dave.

"Mom seemed so tired each night," Sue said. "I think I wanted to lighten her load just a bit, if I could. I would offer to do whatever I could…such as straightening a sheet or some other minor task. I remember how quiet the downstairs was and how soothing the rhythmic sound of the rocking bed was. The up-down-up-down movement was very calming."

While Dave couldn't do much for himself, one thing he eventually could do without help was scratch his nose with the tip of his tongue. "He was so proud of himself," Sue said.

From the beginning, Dave had lots of company when he wasn't too tired. One of the earliest visitors was Al McCartney, co-owner with Charlie Greene of Green and McCartney Allis Chalmers Implements a mile south of Durand. In a visit to Dave nearly a year earlier when he was in Rockford Township Hospital, Al promised him "when you are well enough to be out of the iron lung, I'll bring down the newest tractor to show you."

Keeping his promise in the fall of 1956, Al loaded up a new Allis Chalmers D15 tractor on a trailer and drove it to our farm to show Dave. Mom and Dad pushed Dave in his wheelchair to the middle of the front lawn. Al unloaded the tractor and drove it in circles around Dave, showing off his prized possession. Bill, Bernie and Tom were all in the yard, watching with eyes wide open.

Dave told Al he was going to drive the tractor someday.

"I know you are," Al replied.

In retelling the story later, Al said Dave had said, "If I can't drive the tractor, I can sit in a wheelchair and do the books."

Eventually, Greene and McCartney and the Ford implement

dealership of Leo Spelman brought out new tractors and parked them in the front yard so Dave could see them through the big window.

His best friends from high school — Jack Walsh, Bob Haggerty, Tom Dolan and Norm Chilton — stopped by often too.

"We would shut the glass doors to the room so they could just laugh and visit for as long as Dave wanted them to stay," Julie said. "Jack said Dave cheered him up instead of the other way around."

One of the most faithful visitors was Norm Chilton, who had enrolled that fall at the University of Wisconsin at Whitewater, about 50 miles north of Durand. Every Friday Norm would drive home and then come out from town to visit Dave.

Norm found Dave to be interested in everything he had to say. Dave also was a fountain of information, filling Norm in on all the news of the past week. He looked forward to his weekly visits and getting caught up on all he had missed the previous week.

One Friday Norm arrived at our home and found Dave asleep. He didn't want to wake him so he left. The next Friday Dave informed Norm that if he was ever asleep again when Norm arrived, he should wake him up.

On one of his visits, Norm arrived as Mom and Dad were putting Dave into the back of the station wagon for a trip to Beloit. They invited Norm to join them. He remembers how slow they drove the nearly 20 miles to Beloit and recalls two very old people coming out to the car to visit with Dave. Without knowing it, Norm had just met our Grandpa and Grandma Kenucane.

When Aunt Pat brought Grandpa and Grandma to our house to visit Dave, he always would say, "Turn off the rocking bed because it makes Grandma dizzy."

Cousin Tom Dolan also visited Dave often, sometimes bringing along the high school tape recorder and the play-by-play tapes that he and Dave McCullough made of the previous season's Durand High School basketball games. The team wasn't very good, even though

Norm was the leading scorer, averaging 17.4 points a game. The Bulldogs finished the season with a 7-17 record and ended up third in the Stephenson County Conference with a 4-6 record. Dave didn't care; he loved listening to the games.

Father Driscoll was a frequent visitor too. It was a very special time when he came to the door with the Holy Eucharist and gave communion to Dave and later on to Rose.

"One of us kids would meet him at the door with a lighted candle and back into the big room without tripping over something," Sue said."It was also absolutely quiet — no one was allowed to utter a word. Father would happily stay for breakfast after administering the sacrament."

One morning, as he was sitting down in the chair, Father went crashing to the floor when the chair gave out. He not only was oversized but also possessed a large sense of humor. We were all mortified, especially Mom, but Father just laughed it off, was given a sturdy chair and ate his scrambled eggs.

Our family celebrated Christmas with Dave, who typed a letter to *The Durand Gazette,* which published it on Jan. 10, 1957. It read:

> *"I wish to thank everyone who visited me and sent me cards and gifts which helped make my first Christmas back home a merry one.*
> *"Dave Walsh."*

When friends weren't visiting, we provided Dave with lots of companionship. *The Rockford Register Republic* published a photo on Jan. 19, 1957, of Dave in his room sitting in his wheelchair while Rose and Molly played checkers with him with the board resting on his lap.

Rose liked playing 45 r.p.m. records for Dave on the record player next to his rocking bed. She enjoyed watching the records, such as Fats Domino's hit "Blueberry Hill," drop down onto the turntable.

Giving Dave a bath in his bulky bathtub in the new room was an adventure. The wooden tub, made especially for Dave's special needs, was more than six feet long and four feet wide, about three and a half feet high with strong, straight legs and lined with tin. It reminded Sue of the horse tank outside that was used to water our livestock.

Dave was lifted in and out of the tub with a large, mechanical Hoyer lift. It had a long hydraulic arm, operated by the nurses, which could be moved up and down and sideways. A large canvas sling was placed under Dave in his bed and then hooked to the sturdy arm of steel on the lift. With Dave safe in the sling, the nurses pumped the arm to raise Dave up and off the bed. The entire lift was then rolled to the tub and Dave was slowly lowered into the water.

Dave enjoyed being around most of his nurses. But Mrs. Fowler was a different story. Months after she no longer worked for us, Dad was notified of a lawsuit she had filed, claiming Mom and Dad were negligent and the cause of an auto accident she had while driving home from our place. We didn't even know she had an accident and the lawsuit was dismissed.

Although Dad was tired from working on the farm, he kept an "ear" out during the night for Dave. One night the nurse fell asleep. She awoke to see Dad giving Dave a drink of water. Dad had heard a noise "so I got up to check," he said.

Meanwhile, Rose continued her daily exercises at home and her twice-a-week trips to St. Anthony Hospital for physical therapy treatments. She loved the drives home if only because it meant stopping at Sparky's, a small grocery store on the edge of Rockford. Mom let Rose browse around the store before always picking her favorites, a Bun candy bar or a Twinkie.

Aunt Margaret, a retired teacher, tutored Rose for her regular public school classes as well as for preparation to receive her first Holy Communion.

"Rose started school this year," Mom said. "But doctors told us to take her out. She needs exercise every day. She has curvature of the spine and weak abdominal muscles. We hope she'll be able to go to school next year."

In March 1957, Rose, now 6 years old, was fitted for a Milwaukee Brace in preparation for spinal surgery. It was a full torso brace used in the treatment of spinal curvatures in children. The brace extended from the pelvis to the chin and the back of the head.

About the same time, on March 4, Dave celebrated his 19th birthday with six birthday cakes, many letters and cards and lots of visits from friends and relatives.

Seven weeks later, on April 22, Rose underwent the first of two back surgeries at St. Anthony's Hospital.

"In a three-hour operation, the surgeon took bone splinters from the shin bone in one of her legs and fused them into four of the vertebrae in her back to strengthen them," *The Rockford Morning Star* reported. Later, she had another five vertebrae operated on.

On May 9, *The Durand Gazette* published this item:

"A shower of 'cards' is being suggested for Rose Ellen Walsh, who is a surgery patient at St. Anthony's Hospital in Rockford. P.T.A. members know a remembrance for this little first grade girl would make her days in the hospital more cheery and bright. Won't you write her too?"

The next month, *The Durand Gazette* published three letters from members of our family. They read:

"I wish to thank everyone who visited me or sent me letters, gifts, flowers or cards. I received over 100 cards from the P.T.A. Card Shower.
"Rose Ellen Walsh."

"I wish to thank the many people who visited me and also sent me cards and flowers.
"Dave Walsh."

"We wish to thank the Class of 1957 for the very beautiful
bouquet of white carnations which you placed on Edward's grave.
"The family of Edward Walsh."

The Class of 1957 also dedicated its yearbook to Ed, with the first page displaying his picture above the inscription:

"It is with great reverence that we set aside this page as a memorial to our absent classmate, Ed Walsh. His courage will always be admired by us."

In addition, the Student Council presented the high school a plaque in memory of Ed, which is still hanging today on the wall of the school's main corridor.

Visitors continued to stop by to see Dave. One of the most touching visits was one by Bev Meier and Ken Waller, wearing their wedding clothes. They had been married that morning, June 15, at the Durand Methodist Church, and drove out to our farm to see Dave before they went to their reception at the Meier farm about six miles west of ours. It was a special treat for Dave and all of us.

Five days later, Dave's stay at home ended. Illinois Research Hospital sent a special truck with a portable respirator to take Dave back to Chicago to undergo surgery for kidney stones.

Our family physician, Dr. Leonard, emphasized that the transfer was not an emergency.

"I ordered the truck," he said. "We had been planning to do this work sometime early this summer."

Sheriffs' departments in Winnebago, Boone and McHenry counties escorted the truck, with State Police taking over the duty from the McHenry line to the hospital in Chicago.

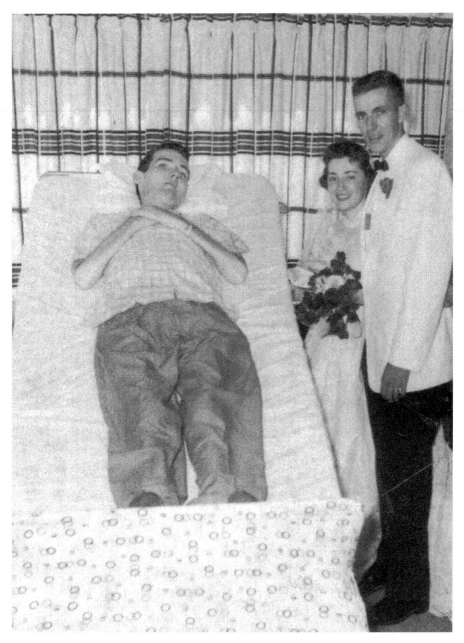

Bev Meier Waller and her husband of a few hours, Ken Waller, visit Dave in his rocking bed at home after their wedding that morning on June 15, 1957. (Photo by Dave McCullough).

In May 1957, Anne, standing at left, and Alice, seated at right, were selected for the Junior Prom Court. (DHS yearbook).

Above, Rose sitting at her desk at home with her doll in early 1957. (Walsh family photo).

Right, Rose in her Milwaukee Brace decorating the Christmas tree with Fran. (Walsh family photo).

CHAPTER 17:

More Broken Hearts

D ave was back in the hospital less than three weeks when Rose, confined to her little bed in the Milwaukee brace, received her First Communion from Father Driscoll in a special ceremony at our home on July 8, 1957. All of her First Communion classmates, dressed in their special white dresses and suits, were there. So was Aunt Margaret.

Dave's stay at Illinois Research Hospital was intended to be brief. The plan was for him to have surgery for kidney stones. But the surgery never occurred because he developed a kidney infection. It progressed rapidly, plunging him into critical condition for several weeks.

He never recovered.

Dave, the fun-loving boy who with his brother Ed invented Bare Ass Beach, who loved racing cars around Durand with his buddies, who was admired by and an inspiration to his many friends and who yearned to be a farmer the rest of his life, died on Tuesday, Sept. 3.

He was not alone. Mom was at his side.

Newspapers reported the time of death as 12:15 p.m. but the death certificate listed it as 11:30 a.m. An autopsy the next day said the immediate cause of death was "chronic pyelonephritis with uremia and bilateral renal calculi," (kidney infection and kidney stones).

Several of Mom's sisters were at our house when Mom came home that evening. "All of us were crying and Mother broke down, wailing and crying uncontrollably," Julie said. "Aunt Teresa comforted her. It was scary. I wondered if Mother would be OK again. She went to bed exhausted and absolutely grief stricken."

The next night many of us went out on the flat gravel roof over the room that had been built for Dave and Ed and watched the brilliantly colored Northern Lights.

"It was like Dave saying to all of us, 'I am finally up here with God, and it is great,'" Anne said.

Anne was especially devastated by Dave's death.

"Dave and I were buddies," she said. "We ran with the same kids in high school and had loads of fun in our big group."

As with Ed's death a year earlier, the planning and work for Dave's wake and funeral began quickly. Once again Father Driscoll and funeral director Floy Chapin were consulted.

Dave was brought from Chicago to the funeral home and then out to our house, where his casket was placed in the same spot where Ed's had rested, against the west wall of the living room. Like Ed's, it was surrounded by flowers and large candles.

The wake was held on Thursday evening, Sept. 5. Bill again served as the Doorman and once again thought the line of people would never end. Once again cars were parked all the way up the hill on both sides of Baker Road.

Father Driscoll again led the praying of the rosary and many in the crowd lingered until later in the evening.

Mom and Dad sat on our davenport, a few feet from Dave, as they greeted mourners. Rose lay across their laps in her brace for a while during the wake. Bernie recalled seeing Dad cry and "wishing he didn't have to do that."

The next morning the casket was loaded into Chapin's hearse and began its journey to Durand and St. Mary's Church. The parade of cars seemed endless. "It was all so final...I thought my heart would break," Anne said.

As Mom entered the church vestibule, she was approached by a reporter. She told him to get out; she said she didn't want to talk to reporters anymore.

Dr. Janet Wolter, who helped take care of Dave at Illinois Research Hospital and loaned her apartment to Mom when she visited, sped much of the way on Route 20 and arrived just as the funeral was beginning. Despite being late, she did have a chance to speak with Mom and Dad.

During the Mass, our cousin Jerry, who was still studying for the priesthood, told Mom and Anne that he saw the reflection of the Virgin Mary ceiling mural on top of Dave's casket.

After the funeral, the casket was taken to St. Mary's cemetery and Dave was buried next to Ed.

Once again, mourners returned to our home for a meal served by our sisters and women from St. Mary's.

And once again, very few people years later remembered any details of the visitation or funeral service. The altar boys were Tom Dolan, Mike Dolan, Bob Haggerty and Dan Waller. Other classmates were probably pall bearers, but no one could say for sure who they all were. Jack Walsh thinks he was one, but wasn't sure. Only one person, Aunt Margaret's son Jim Walsh, was certain that two of the pall bearers were Tom Spelman and Dave's classmate Bill Rogers.

Forgetting the details of Dave and Ed's ordeal and deaths was common. Many folks remembered visiting Dave and Ed in their iron lungs at our home. But they are mistaken — Dave and Ed were never in the room together. Once Ed was hospitalized in September 1955, he never returned home. And there was never an iron lung in our home.

Perhaps in people's memories our two brothers, Dave and Ed, have blended into one person, "Dave'n'Ed." Perhaps the years have played tricks on many aging people's memories. Or perhaps the entire ordeal was so traumatic that people blocked out much of the detail.

That week John R. Van Sickle, the owner and editor of *The Durand Gazette*, saluted Dave in his front-page column. It said:

"Although death appeared to have won the victory on Tuesday, David Walsh, in reality was the victor for he had conquered even death with his soaring spirit that keep fighting for long months against the crippling disease that was wasting him away.

"His loved ones and his many, many friends will never forget the courageous outlook that David maintained in his losing struggle that extended over long, long months of rocking beds, respirators, hospital beds and hours and hours of pain.

"The memory of David's determination and grit cannot be erased by the quietness of death. His spirit still marches on in the lives of those who knew him."

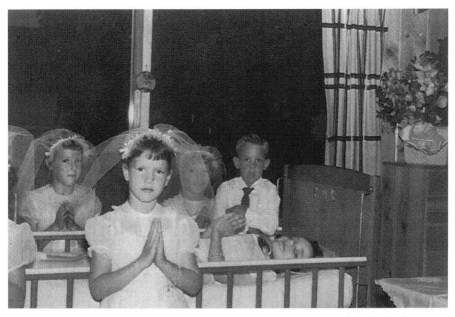

Rose in her bed at her first communion service in Dave's Room on July 8, 1957. With her are Judy Gaffney, foreground, and in the back, from left, Deb Sweet, Kathy Meissen and Jim Thomas. (Walsh family photo).

Father Jerry Walsh, our cousin, who told Mom and Anne that he saw the reflection of the Virgin Mary ceiling mural on Dave's casket at his funeral. (Walsh family photo).

IN MEMORIAM

It is with great reverence that we set aside this page as a memorial to our absent classmate, Ed Walsh. His courage will always be admired by us.

Both Ed and Dave's (following page) classes at Durand High School dedicated their yearbooks to them. (DHS yearbook).

Dedication

To you, David Walsh, one of our most active class members, we dedicate this Medina. We, the Senior Class of 1956, hope that in this very small way we can show our appreciation for your friendship and our admiration for your courage.

CHAPTER 18:

Tom Dolan's Poem

While both Dave and Ed got hundreds of cards and letters throughout their illness, one of the most heartfelt, in the form of a poem dedicated to Dave, didn't arrive at our house while Dave was alive.

The poem was written over several months by our cousin Tom Dolan.

Tom and Dave each considered the other to be his best friend. Tom started writing the poem shortly after Dave contracted polio in September 1955. He wrote other verses after Dave was admitted to Illinois Research Hospital in Chicago.

At the same time Tom also began taking guitar lessons from Olive Crowley, who Mom had hired years earlier to give piano lessons to our twin sisters, Alice and Anne and Joan and Julie. Tom often played the guitar outside sitting under the big tree in the Dolans' front yard, singing the words of his poem. Sixty years later Tom still played the same guitar.

Shortly after Dave died, Tom's mother, Aunt Ellen, discovered the poem when she spotted a piece of paper peeking out of an encyclopedia in the family's study room. She asked Tom if she could save it. He was embarrassed that she discovered it and told her to "leave it where she found it. But she was insistent that she wanted it so I told her she could have it."

Years later the poem, with the two last verses written most likely by Aunt Ellen, resurfaced. Aunt Ellen probably had given it to Mom. It was a stirring tribute to Dave:

COUSIN DAVE

Tall, dark and handsome; age seventeen;
Hard working farm boy with a good future foreseen.
His friends, he had many, his enemies none.
His way of living was exciting, reckless and fun!
Easy going in a very casual way,
Never worrying or wondering about the next day!
  Cousin Dave, a gay young man.
  Cousin Dave with a dark sun tan.
  Cousin Dave over six foot tall.
  Cousin Dave loved by all!
Typical youth throughout the land.

Then at the end of an early autumn day,
He became ill and about half asleep he lay.
His headache grew worse and his fever way high.
His neck got stiff and his mouth was dry.
He knew he was sick, but he didn't know;
That his illness was caused by polio!
  Cousin Dave in a hospital lay.
  Cousin Dave about to pass away.
  Cousin Dave's life was dim.
  Cousin Dave's chances were slim.
There was nothing left to do but pray!

Dropped like a mighty oak from a woodman's ax;
He was as strong as the oak itself,
But now lay there as motionless and helpless
As a book on the shelf!

The crisis was over and his stout heart held out;
But the damage was done and his future in doubt.
  Cousin Dave had one battle won!
  Cousin Dave was fighting the other one.
  Cousin Dave's spirits were high.
  Cousin Dave wouldn't say die!
Who would be victor when the battle was won?

Life to his muscles and tendons were never restored.
And through operations and therapy he never seemed bored.
He always was gay and his wit and humor was keen.
But we will never know what pain and agony there had been!
  Cousin Dave fought on and on.
  Cousin Dave's hope wasn't gone!
  Cousin Dave in his sick bed lay.
Was he fighting a battle that couldn't be won?

As time went by and years numbered nearly two;
Cousin Dave had grown worse and death was in view!
Gray was the sky, a chilly wind blew;
And a few teardrops of rain fell from the sky.
The world seemed to mourn, and the sun didn't shine.
That was the time Cousin Dave must have died!
  Cousin Dave was again set free!
  Cousin Dave for eternity.
  Cousin Dave is ahead of us all!
  Cousin Dave had gotten his call.
Which one of us next will Cousin Dave see?

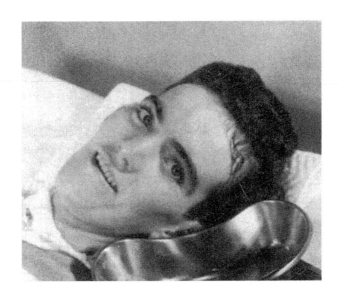

CHAPTER 19:

How Did We Defeat Polio?

S ome people may think we didn't defeat polio. After all, we lost two of our brothers to the dreaded disease. But Mom and Dad picked up the pieces of their broken, grief-stricken hearts and continued caring for their other 12 children. They could have crumbled and said they wouldn't be able to continue farming without Dave and Ed. But they chose another path, the one to rebuilding their lives.

This "recovery" happened because our parents, like their parents before them, were guided along that path by their strong faith. It gave them strength to continue to live their Irish Catholic "busy-but-never-too-busy-for-nightly-prayers-and-weekly-Mass" way of life.

We did it by clinging to our faith.

And by praying every day.

And by knowing thousands of people were praying every day.

And with enormous support from family and friends, especially Dad's nephews and Mom's sisters.

And with expert guidance and advice from Father Driscoll and Dr. Leonard.

Not that there weren't times of despair throughout the siege.

"Once, on a cold winter day, Dad came into the kitchen with tears in his eyes and sat down, unable to hold back his grief," Julie said. His two sons were seriously ill, his calves were dying and he didn't have enough help.

"Mother put her arms around his shoulders, they talked quietly and I heard Mother tell him that things would be all right," Julie added. "He stayed briefly, got up and went back outside to his work."

Julie also recalled Dad being frustrated after returning from a trip to town to buy some groceries. With tears in his eyes, he said, "Everyone keeps asking about the boys and I have to keep telling them the same thing. They are the same, they are not good."

Another time Dad, in a moment of grief, said he was thinking about selling the farm now that both of his oldest sons were gone. But he quickly realized that he had three other outstanding sons.

Years later, Mom told her teen-aged grandson, Chris Cocoma, about one of her moments of despair.

When Molly was taken to the hospital after injuring her eye, Mom tried to visit her in the emergency room. But the ER staff stopped her, saying it would be too upsetting for Molly to see Mom.

"Grandma couldn't take anymore," Chris said. "At that moment she asked God to leave her children alone and take her. She told God she would gladly die for any of her children. She implored Him to take her."

After the crisis, Mom had to deal with a different kind of despair. In the spring and summer of 1958, she was plagued with severe debilitating headaches. Today she most likely would be treated for migraines and possibly for Post Traumatic Stress Disorder. Her painful headaches gradually became less frequent but persisted for years.

Nevertheless, Mom and Dad were pillars of strength throughout the crisis.

Just ask Lorraine: "Mom and Dad were able to cope with the nightmare because of their faith."

Or Anne: "The prayers that were sent up to Heaven are probably what kept us all sane."

Or Alice: "How we prayed the rosary…we prayed it every night. Dad down on his knees, too. What an example!"

Or Joan: "Mom and Dad certainly earned their (angel) 'wings' after suffering through those polio years. Shows what a strong faith they had and (they) did a wonderful job of passing it on to their children."

Or Julie: "Where could Mother and Dad have found the strength and serenity to accept God's will for them without the help of prayer and their faith? They never gave up their faith or let themselves be totally overcome by sorrow. They maintained their sense of humor… they continued fervent, quiet prayer."

Or Aunt Margaret: "Her deep faith sustained your Mom. She was admirable…your father was wonderful. Even after he lost his two teen-aged sons he carried on courageously."

Or Mary Lou Walsh, Aunt Margaret's daughter and our cousin: "I think our families were welded together because of the helplessness we all felt…I never heard your Mom say one word about those years when they were over…she put on many hats, whatever one was needed for each child. At home she would go upstairs for her sick ones, giving love and support to each one. Then she would go to the hospital to support those there…Once she was sitting on the back steps with me and I told her just to stay there. She said, 'There is no time for me—I can't rest. They need me.' No one ever knew how she did it. I'm sure she got her strength from God. She never showed any bitterness and accepted her cross…so did your Dad…there is an inner strength that we all could use if we just had her faith."

Perhaps Mom herself summed it up best many years later when asked by her son-in-law, Bill Landers, how she was able to cope and survive during the polio crisis:

"We did what we had to do.

"We learned to accept what you can and can't change.

"We took one day at a time.

"We had lots of support from our family, friends and our church. Faith was especially important.

"It was important to keep our sense of humor, finding something to smile and laugh about.

"I still found time to read novels, do gardening and write letters."

And then Mom added a final story.

"I remember once reading a book called *Mrs. Mike.* The main character grew up with many privileges. She ended up moving to the Canadian wilderness, getting married and having a family; life was difficult. Mrs. Mike sometimes reflected on the times she used to complain about "burnt toast and spilled milk" and now how trivial this was in comparison to her current life. It gave her perspective on what is important. I would sometimes think about this book and its message, and it helped me."

CHAPTER 20:

Life Resumes

After Dave died, life returned to a different normal. The special room built for "the boys" became known as Dave's Room. All of his medical equipment was quietly moved out except for his long bathtub. It was disconnected from the water pipes and moved under the big corner windows. Mom converted it to a winter flower garden, displaying a variety of potted plants, including the big geraniums she brought inside in the fall. In the summer the tub was moved outside, making a perfect outdoor swimming pool for the three little girls.

In the fall of 1957, Alice and Anne were busy seniors at Durand High School. Alice was editor of the yearbook and Anne was vice president of the class and president of the Future Homemakers of America. The motto for FHA that year was "Forward Ever, Backward Never."

Fifth-grader Bernie took his place on the farm chore crew and second-grader Rose continued to be tutored at home by Aunt Margaret. After that school year, Rose was able to attend school and, despite her limitations, got around quite well.

On a cold Sunday in January 1958, Otter Creek was once again the venue for teen-agers at play. Our four twins hosted a skating party for their high school friends. It was Mom and Dad's way of saying "thank you" for supporting us and our girls during the last three years. The ice was slick and smooth near Bare Donkey Beach, which was in the prime skating area. The skaters, some of whom skated the two miles east to the Sugar River, walked back to our house for hot cocoa, sandwiches and doughnuts. Dave's Room was filled with the laughter of happy kids; it was music to all our ears.

Lorraine and Bob Vormezeele were engaged in April 1958 and a month later Father Jerry was ordained a priest. Lorraine shopped for her wedding dress by herself because Mom was in the hospital undergoing tests to determine the cause of her recent headaches. Lorraine made Molly's gold flower-girl dress for the wedding. It was the same style as Alice and Anne's bridesmaid dresses.

On Sept. 20, 1958, Lorraine and Bob were married at St. Mary's with Father Driscoll officiating, after which they joined all their guests at the reception at the Swiss Wheel in Monroe, Wis. They returned to our house to change their clothes and then left for their honeymoon to the West Coast.

The morning of the ceremony *The Rockford Morning Star* published a sizable story about the wedding and on Sunday published three large wedding photos across the entire eight columns of Page B1 above the masthead. Mom told the *Star* reporter that after this event, "We want no more news coverage. Please leave our family alone now."

Lorraine wasn't the only daughter to leave home that fall. Alice enrolled in St. Anthony's School of Nursing. She had decided to be a nurse while helping Dave when he was at home. Anne also planned to leave. She was accepted at the Congregation of Sisters of St. Agnes in Fond du Lac, Wis. However, because of Mom's lingering illness, Anne decided to stay home to help her.

"I think all the sickness and stress since 1955 were too much for her," Anne said. During her year at home Anne changed her mind about the convent. In the fall of 1959, Anne and Julie joined Alice at nursing school. Joan chose another way to help people and enrolled in the flight attendant program at McConnell Airline School in Minneapolis.

Autumn was a melancholy time for Mom. Each year when the leaves changed she thought of how her hope that "the boys" would fully recover had faded as the leaves fell in 1955. She could never stand to listen to the song "Autumn Leaves" again.

Each year when Alice sees a big orange moon in the fall, she thinks of an evening ride home from Township Hospital after visiting Dave and Ed. That's when she saw the same kind of moon, and Dad told her it was a harvest moon.

Bill graduated from Durand High School in 1962 after displaying some of Ed's athletic skills on the basketball court. Coach Sid Felder said Bill, as the sixth man, was one of the most valuable players on the team that compiled the school's best record of 25-2.

Bill also displayed some of Dave's showmanship skills in August 1963 when he achieved what Dave and Ed never did—he showed the Grand Champion steer at the Winnebago County 4-H Fair. This was possibly one of the happiest days of Dad's life. A steer from his beloved, tenderly cared-for Black Angus herd was awarded the coveted purple ribbon.

Before the steer was auctioned, Dad told a *Morning Star* reporter that "we'll be satisfied if Bill gets 80 cents or so a pound." The steer, weighing 1,065 pounds, sold for a record $1.20 a pound, breaking the 1959 mark by 27 cents a pound. The purchase of $1,278 was made by the First National Bank and Trust Co. in Rockford.

The exciting day was not without reminders of the polio years.

The first thing Mom did when she arrived home from the fair was to call Milwaukee Children's Hospital, where Rose was a patient. Two weeks earlier, Rose, then 12, underwent seven hours of spinal surgery. When the nurse relayed Mom's message about the winning steer to her, Rose had a few happy tears. She knew how much the top prize at the fair meant to our family, and wished she could have been there.

Instead Rose again was confined to bed for another six months, in another Milwaukee Brace, after another spinal fusion. The fusions done in 1957 had not been successful, and once again her spine had begun to curve.

Dr. Leonard had referred Rose to Dr. Walter Blount, the inventor of the Milwaukee Brace. Dr. Blount's office was a few blocks from Children's Hospital, which was about a two-hour drive from our farm. At Rose's first appointment, the doctor quickly wrote orders for a new brace, which was made in Rockford. After the brace was worn for one month, the complex surgery was performed. This time the bone to reinforce Rose's vertebrae was taken from her ribs. During Rose's one-month hospital stay, Mom often took the train from Durand to Milwaukee to visit her.

Rose spent the next six months in a hospital bed set up in Dave's Room. She was tutored at home for eighth grade. One of her teachers was Cres Vale, the wife of Harry Vale, who remembered Rose as brilliant. "She taught herself," Cres said. "She was a delight to work with."

Rose was able to start high school in 1964, wearing her Milwaukee Brace. The school desks were not comfortable for Rose so a small table with two chairs became her desk. Her friend since first grade, Judy Johnson, enjoyed her time with Rose at the table in Mr. Wilhelmi's English classroom. Judy doesn't remember any distinct examples of their "goofiness," but humor was never in short supply when the two girls were together.

In the years that followed, eventually all of us were married. We returned often to the farm, where our young children had fun playing together, seeing the animals and farm machinery. After Dad died in 1976, Mom moved to Durand. Her younger grandchildren had fun exploring her ranch-style home, with its little pink bathroom and laundry chute.

After Mom's death in August 1987, we decided we wanted to honor our parents' strong sense of family and faith. In 1991 we hired sculptor John Sharp to carve a statue of the Holy Family to honor them.

We selected a huge fallen white oak tree weighing more than 2,000 pounds from our farm near Otter Creek and hauled it to Sharp's studio in Mineral Point, Wis. Using a small clay model for which Bernie, Joan and Tom's daughter Sarah posed, Sharp spent the next two years carving out Jesus, Mary and Joseph. The finished statue weighed about 450 pounds.

On July 18, 1993, all 12 of us surviving brothers and sisters, 36 of Dad and Mom's 41 grandchildren and all 14 of their great grandchildren gathered at St. Mary's Church to celebrate a special Mass and dedicate the white oak sculpture. Today the statue still stands in an alcove in the back east corner of the church.

A plaque at the base of the statue reads:

"In loving memory of our parents, Keron and Anne Walsh, and our brothers, David and Edward."

Bill Walsh with his Grand Champion steer at the Winnebago County 4-H Fair in August 1963. (The Rockford Morning Star).

Sculptor John Sharp's statue of the Holy Family dedicated to Mom and Dad and Dave and Ed at a special Mass at St. Mary's on July 18, 1993. The statue stands in an alcove in the back east corner of the church. (Photo by John Cocoma).

CHAPTER 21:

Whatever Happened to All of Us?

KERON WALSH: Dad lived another 20 years, remaining the devoted, dedicated man he was during our polio crisis. He dedicated himself to his land/farm and church/community until he died in 1976.

When asked if he enjoyed the peace and quiet of the "empty nest" years, tears filled his eyes and he said he missed having all the children running around and having fun playing in the yard like they used to.

He faithfully attended elementary school programs, band concerts, high school plays and other school events until Molly graduated in 1971.

He was a devoted fan of the Durand High School Bulldogs and especially enjoyed watching Bill, Bernie and Tom compete in basketball, football and track. After the boys graduated, he was happy to take Rose, Fran and Molly to the games.

Dad was proud when his grandchildren started school in Durand in the late 1960s. He was delighted when all of us gathered on Christmas afternoon and the house was once more filled with little children "running around."

The 4-H Fair remained the highlight of Dad's summer. Much to his delight, Molly took over as his "showman" in 1967 when Tom turned 18. Dad's Angus steers were proudly shown in the beef ring until 1970, when he turned operation of the farm over to Bill, Bernie and Tom. Bill farmed with Dad when Bernie and Tom went away to school and served in the military before their return to farming.

Dad continued to help the boys every day. Although he was free to leave, he remained reluctant to leave his farm for more than one night, much preferring day trips. Mom did convince him to take two longer excursions, both to visit one of us. The first was in 1968 to New Mexico to visit Anne and her husband, Foster, who was in the Air Force. The other was a train trip in 1973 to visit Rose in Philadelphia, where she was in school.

While in Philly, they took the train to Washington, D.C. Dad had never been there, and was moved to tears while viewing the Lincoln Memorial. He climbed the many steps and paused to study the huge statue of Abe. Dad then sat on the steps, pointed back at Lincoln and, with his voice breaking, said: "He was just a farm boy from Illinois." He then wiped away his tears.

Dad also was just an Irish farm boy who was proud to call Durand (and Laona Township) Illinois home. He was an enthusiastic supporter of all that was good about Durand, including St. Mary's. In the late 1960s and early 1970s he thoroughly enjoyed the church's Harvest Ball, held each Thanksgiving weekend. He invited all his married daughters to attend and reveled in the excitement of that big evening.

He remained active in the community, serving on the School Board from 1958-1970. He loved community celebrations and participated in a skit for the Durand Bicentennial pageant in July 1976. He even joined the girls in a can-can dance for a short time at the end of the show. The crowd loved it.

On Aug. 12, 1976, Dad died suddenly and unexpectedly from a heart attack while working with Bill in the farmyard, on the farm Dad's father had purchased in 1883, the farm Dad lived on all of his life.

His funeral was held Aug. 14, 1976 at St. Mary's with burial in St. Mary Cemetery next to the graves of his sons Dave and Ed. He was survived by his wife, Anne, 12 children, 26 grandchildren and his brother, Leonard.

ANNE CECELIA KENUCANE WALSH: Mom lived another 30

years after 1957. She remained the devoted nurturer and teacher to her children while dealing with her grief. Her resilience in the aftermath of the polio, and later Dad's death, was an example to all of us and others of how to keep going when the pain of losing a loved one makes it feel as if you can't. As we grew and began to leave home, her nurturing roles grew too.

Like Dad, she had fond memories of when their family was young. She often said, "The best time was when the kids were little. I could fix all of their problems. As they grew up, so did their problems." Molly started first grade in 1959, which meant there were no longer any preschoolers at home with Mom. However, she still had 11 people to feed, so her workload didn't lighten much.

All of the children were in extracurricular activities, sports, music lessons, band, 4-H and religious education classes. Mom encouraged us to pursue our interests and attended all of our school performances. She drove many, many miles chauffeuring us to and from town.

In September 1958, Mom took on two new roles: mother of the bride and mother-in-law. We were all excited when Lorraine married Bob Vormezeele at St. Mary's with Father Driscoll officiating. Finally, a fall season with a joyous celebration.

One by one, the older children married. The 1960s were Mom's "wedding planning" decade, with weddings in 1963, '64, '65, '66 and '67. Each one was at St. Mary's. Mom was careful to follow the rules of etiquette with each engagement and wedding. She shopped with care for her mother-of-the-bride outfits, usually choosing a pretty suit. Her stylish accessories — hat, shoes and gloves — also were chosen carefully.

Equally exciting was the arrival of grandchildren, with Number 1 arriving in 1959. Number 41 arrived in 1987, three months before "Grandma Walsh" died. She loved her role as nurturing grandmother and couldn't wait to hold each infant. Her first great grandchild was born in 1981.

Ever the teacher, she decided to teach her grandchildren, even the unborn ones, about "those that came before them." In 1975, Dad and Mom gave each of us a handwritten book of our Walsh and Kenucane family histories. Mom wrote every word in the book. In the introduction, she wrote: "Our love of family prompted us to write what we know of each of our families…our grandchildren one day might be interested in the origin of their ancestors. It is our hope that they will then remember their loving grandparents, Anne and Keron Walsh."

As we left home Mom had more time for her role as sister. In the late 1960s and early 1970s, she enjoyed hosting her family in mid-December for an early Christmas celebration. She took a special interest with her sister of special needs, Kitty. Mom was always looking for craft activities to teach Kitty. In 1958 Mom traveled to Portland, Ore. with her sisters Teresa and Margaret, her niece Mary Lou and Lorraine, to attend the celebration for Sister Emelia, their Kenucane cousin, and her 50 years as a nun.

Mom's faith remained a priority for her and she took time to nurture it. After she moved to town in 1977, she expanded her role as a faithful parish member and led a Bible study group. She would prepare ahead of time so she could lead the discussions around her table in the group of about six women, including Aunt Margaret.

Mom blended her love of flowers with her faith when she added an 18-inch white statue of The Blessed Virgin Mary to her backyard perennial garden on the farm. Dad helped her make a simple "backdrop" for Mary out of cement and pretty rocks, and she was proud to call it her shrine.

Mom's last new role, that of a widow, was suddenly thrust upon her when Dad died in August 1976. Even though she remained active and carried on in the 11 years without Dad, she missed him every day. She often commented that she was "just waiting to be with him again."

Mom remained healthy until contacting a fatal kidney infection and died a day after admission to Rockford Memorial Hospital. All 12 of us were at her bedside in the early morning hours of Aug. 25, 1987. When the last one of us arrived, she said: "Now we can eat," nurturing until the end. When she asked if we could see "the beautiful light," God called her home. Her funeral Mass was held at St. Mary's and burial was at St. Mary Cemetery, next to Dad, and Dave and Ed.

LORRAINE WALSH VORMEZEELE: DHS class of 1955. After graduation from high school, Lorraine stayed home to help during the polio crisis. She was employed as an office worker in Rockford until her marriage in 1958 to Robert Vormezeele, a farmer in business with his father and brother just a few miles from our farm. Eventually, as they acquired additional acreage, Bob and one of his sons formed a farm partnership. Lorraine devoted herself to the care of their six children, Ellen, Jane, Sarah, Francis, John and Beth. They have 17 grandchildren and two great grandchildren. They are retired and live on their farm just east of Durand. Lorraine was named Catholic Woman of the Year for St. Mary's and Irish Grove parishes for 2016.

ANNE WALSH COLBY: DHS class of 1958. Anne graduated from St. Anthony Hospital School of Nursing in 1962 and worked in Madison and Milwaukee hospitals as a staff and/or head nurse until her marriage to Foster Colby in 1967. They lived in New Mexico for two years during which time Foster practiced dentistry while in the Air Force. After moving to Wisconsin in 1969, Foster continued to practice dentistry for another 36 years in Madison, retiring in 2005. They are parents of three children, Jennifer, Christopher and Elizabeth, and grandparents of 11. Madison is still their home for most of the year except during winter when they escape to their home in Scottsdale, Ariz.

ALICE WALSH KRAISS: DHS class of 1958. After graduation from St. Anthony Hospital School of Nursing in 1961, Alice worked in a Madison hospital until joining a Carmelite Convent in Iowa. However, because of health issues, Alice left Carmel before taking final vows. She then worked as a nurse educator at St. Anthony Hospital and years later was on the staff at a nursing home. In 1970, she married Fred Kraiss, who was employed as a grants coordinator for the state of Illinois. They raised four children, Kevin, Daniel, Katherine and Theresa, while living in Rockton, Ill. After retirement, they moved to Shorewood, Wis., where they now live near one of their daughters. They have eight grandchildren.

JOAN WALSH DIDIER: DHS class of 1959. Joan graduated from McConnell Airline School in Minneapolis in 1960 and worked as a bookkeeper in a Rockford medical clinic until her marriage to Jerome Didier in 1963. During their 49 years of marriage, they lived in Rockford and worked in the Didier Greenhouses, a family business. They are the parents of four children, Matthew, Michele, Jacqueline and Andrew, and the grandparents of six. After Jerome's death in 2012, one of their sons assumed management of the now third-generation family business. Joan lives in Rockford near two of their children.

JULIA WALSH WILLKOM: DHS class of 1959. Julie graduated from St. Anthony Hospital School of Nursing in 1962. She worked at times as a public health, industrial and/or hospital staff nurse in Madison. She married Frank Willkom in 1964 and moved to Sun Prairie, Wis., where Frank practiced law for 43 years while also serving as Sun Prairie Municipal Judge for 38 years. They are the parents of three children, Franz, Jeanne and Colleen, and the grandparents of four. After Frank's death in 2012, Julie moved to Greendale, Wis. to be near her children.

SUE WALSH COCOMA: (See details in "About the Authors" section).

BILL WALSH: DHS class of 1962. After graduation, Bill worked with Dad on the farm and also for the Winnebago County Highway Department. He married Denise Bielema in 1975. He is the father of two children, Phillip and Paulette, from a previous marriage to Nancy

McCartney, and became the adoptive father of Denise's daughter, Jodi. They have eight grandchildren and one great grandchild. A granddaughter, Lucy Walsh, died in a plane accident in 2011 at age 14. Deni is retired from office work and Bill from the highway department. Bill continues to help Bernie in the business of farming and seed sales. They live on their farm about a mile from our home farm.

BERNARD WALSH: DHS class of 1965. Bernie served in the Air Force for four years, beginning in 1967, as a mechanic for support equipment in the Philippines, Vietnam and Thailand. He completed college courses in agriculture and aviation technology and returned to farming the home farm in 1973, working with Bill and Tom in livestock, corn and soybean production. He married Deborah O'Keefe in 1976 and they became the parents of three sons, Brian, Andrew and David. Livestock production was gradually phased out on the farm and ended by the year 2000. Bernie also harvested crops for other area farmers. In 2000, he began work with Syngenta, selling seeds, a business that has been expanded and now includes treating soybeans prior to their sale. Deb, now retired, was a special education and reading teacher in Durand. Bernie continues farming full-time in addition to managing the seed business. They have five grandchildren.

TOM WALSH: DHS class of 1967. Tom attended the University of Illinois and then served from 1970 to 1972 as an Army Ranger in South Korea. After military duty, he returned to farming for five years, then worked as a real-estate appraiser in Rockford. He married Julie Gugerty in 1973. The live on their farm in what was once Aunt Daisy's home just up Baker Road from our home farm. Julie retired in 2013 as a teacher and school librarian. Tom is currently the Supervisor of Assessments for Winnebago County. They are the parents of three daughters, Amy, Laura and Sarah, and have five grandchildren.

ROSE WALSH LANDERS: (See details in "About the Authors"

section).

FRANCES WALSH MCGINNIS: DHS class of 1970. After graduating in 1974 from Western Illinois University with a degree in fashion merchandising and business, Fran worked in retail as a buyer while living in Rockford. She later moved to Chicago and began a career in real-estate sales. She married Joseph McGinnis in 1993. They have no children. They enjoy sailing and their 100-plus nieces and nephews. Joe is a real-estate attorney in Chicago and Fran is a Realtor with Caldwell Banker Lincoln Park Plaza Residential Brokerage serving Chicago and surrounding areas.

MOLLY WALSH JOHNSON: DHS class of 1971. Molly became our fourth sister to graduate from St. Anthony Hospital School of Nursing in 1974 and worked as an intensive care unit nurse in Rockford until her marriage to Phil Johnson in 1975. She has practiced neo-natal and pediatric intensive-care nursing in Iowa and Wisconsin in addition to performing clinic work with an orthopedic surgeon in Appleton, Wis. She and Phil live in Winneconne, Wis., where Phil has practiced veterinary medicine for 35 years. They have four children, Emily, Paul, Mark and Beth, and are the grandparents of five.

SUSAN (MAXWELL) AND THOMAS KENUCANE: Grandma and Grandpa Kenucane died one year apart, Grandma at age 82 in 1961 and Grandpa at age 93 in 1962. They both died at home under the loving care of their family, especially Aunts Pat and Teresa. Their funerals were at St. Jude Catholic Church in Beloit with burials in Mt. Olivet Cemetery in Janesville, Wis. Nine of their 13 children were born when they lived on their farm near Janesville before moving to Beloit.

AUNT DAISY (MARY) WALSH (Dad's sister): Aunt Daisy continued living a quiet life attending to her many African violet house plants. We always stopped at her house to give her a ride to Mass or to run errands. Eventually, she lived with Mother and Dad and at times with Aunt Margaret and Uncle Leonard. She remained an active member of St. Mary's parish until she died at age 88 in 1973.

AUNT MARGARET (Mom's sister) AND UNCLE LEONARD (Dad's brother): Aunt Margaret and Uncle Leonard built a ranch-style home in Durand in the mid-1950s. Uncle Leonard continued farming with their son Joe. Welcoming their grandchildren, attending the ordination and first Mass of their son, Father Jerry, and celebrating their 50th wedding anniversary were some of their greatest joys. They were active, lifelong members of St. Mary's. Uncle Leonard, who outlived all of his siblings, died in 1980 at age 86. Aunt Margaret died in 1992 at age 90.

FATHER MATTHIAS WALSH: Our cousin Jerry was ordained in 1958 and took Matthias as his religious name. We considered him very adventurous when he chose to be a foreign missionary and was assigned to Nigeria in 1959, where he worked in various Dominican ministries for the next 20 years. He helped to found the Dominican Province now existing in Nigeria. He preached for the next several years in missions in the American Midwest, spent several years in Papua, New Guinea and then became the director of St. Jude Shrine in Chicago. He spent the last years of his life doing limited ministry work in Madison, where he died at age 81 in 2013 and is buried in Resurrection Cemetery.

MARY LOU WALSH: Mary Lou remained a single "working girl," living in town with her folks. She was secretary at Doty Motors in Durand for many years and later worked in a facility for troubled youth in Rockford. She was well-known for her fun-loving personality, her great bowling skills (she won several tournaments over the years) and extensive volunteer work. She enjoyed traveling, especially her trips to Ireland. She was named Catholic Woman of the Year in 1995 for St.

Mary's and Irish Grove parishes. She died at age 74 in 2004.

JOE WALSH: Joe continued farming with his dad and worked also as a school bus driver. He and his wife Florence (Rowley) Walsh raised their three children, Donald, Patricia and Janet, in the home where Joe grew up not far from our farm home. Joe and Florence remained active members of St. Mary's. Their son Donald, father of two sons, died at age 45 in 1998. Joe and "Flo" have four grandchildren and one great grandchild. Joe died at age 83 in 2010. Florence is still very active at age 91.

JIM WALSH: Jim and his wife Barbara (Graham) Walsh lived, worked and raised their three children, Dennis, Terrance and Mary Jo, in Beloit, Wis. They are grandparents of five and have two great grandchildren. Jim and Barb are members of St. Jude Catholic Church in Beloit.

MARIAN WALSH AND AUNT NITA WALSH: Marian moved into town and remained a single "working girl" in Rockford. She brought Aunt Nita (Uncle Jay's widow) from her home in Chicago to live with her until Aunt Nita's admission to Medina Nursing Home in Durand, where she died in 2002, just three weeks before her 100th birthday. Both were active members of St. Mary's parish. Marian lived her final days at Medina and died in 2011 at age 80.

BOB WALSH: Bob continued farming with his dad, George, on Walsh Road. He married Jean Losiewski in 1955, just a few months before the beginning of our polio crisis. They raised five children, Michael, Valerie, Teresa, Stephen and Kathleen, and became grandparents of seven. Bob died at age 70 in 2000. Jean lives in Durand and remains an active member of St. Mary's.

AUNT MARY MULCAHY (Mom's sister): Aunt Mary and Uncle Max remained on the Mulcahy family farm in Footville, Wis. until moving to Janesville in their later years. Aunt Mary often drove to Durand for visits to offer Mom support. They were active members of St. Augustine parish in Footville. Aunt Mary died at age 79 in 1979, 11 years before Uncle Max's death in 1990.

AUNT TERESA HOUGHTON (Mom's sister): Aunt Teresa and Uncle Bill lived in Beloit and adopted two sons, James and Mark. Teresa eventually resumed her nursing career and continued to lend a great deal of support to Mom. Uncle Bill died in 1993. Their son James died at age 50 in 2003 and Aunt Teresa died at age 88 in 2005. All three funerals were held at St. Jude's Catholic Church in Beloit, the city in which Mark still lives.

AUNT PAT KENUCANE (Mom's sister): Aunt Pat never married and lived in Beloit with her aging parents, our bachelor uncles Joe and Phil Kenucane and their developmentally disabled sister, Aunt Kitty. After the death of her parents and brothers, the Kenucane farms were sold and Aunt Pat moved with Aunt Kitty to a home in Beloit. Aunt Pat did extensive volunteer work for St. Jude parish and Beloit civic organizations. She lived her final years in the same Beloit extended care facility where her sisters, Teresa and Katherine, lived before their deaths. Aunt Pat died at age 93 in 2015.

UNCLE LAURENCE AND AUNT ELLEN DOLAN (Mom's sister): In 1951, Uncle Laurence and Aunt Ellen moved their family of four children, Mary Therese, Tom, Mike and Charlotte, from the Dolan Homestead just up Baker Road from Aunt Daisy's and the Dolan School, to a second Dolan farm on Highway 75 about two miles southeast of Durand. Uncle Laurence continued to farm both farms with his sons. He was active in the Farm Bureau, served many years on the Durand School Board and was an usher at St. Mary's for decades. Although Aunt Ellen was in declining health for several years, she was active in St. Mary Sodality. She died at age 66 in 1974 and Uncle

Laurence died at age 74 in 1979. Both are buried in St. Mary Cemetery.

MARY THERESE DOLAN: DHS class of 1955: Mary attended Edgewood College for three years and in 1958 entered the Sinsinawa Dominican Convent in Sinsinawa, Wis. She was professed in 1960, received her bachelor's degree from Edgewood, began her teaching career in elementary education and advanced to administrative positions. Sister Mary eventually earned a master's degree in education/reading specialist and a second master's degree in religious studies. This led to her becoming Director of Parish Ministries, Faith Formation and RCIA Programs in various parishes, with which she continues to be involved today. She lives in Madison.

TOM DOLAN: DHS class of 1956: After graduation, Tom remained on the family farm. He was drafted into the Army in 1961, trained as a heavy-equipment operator and served two years active duty and four years in the reserves. In 1970, he married Geraldine McMorrough in Dublin, Ireland. Although divorced, they raised three sons and are grandparents of nine. Tom and his brother Mike farmed together until 1990. Tom served on many farm boards and was involved with his sons' many activities, including 4-H. He remains active in St. Mary's parish.

MIKE DOLAN: DHS class of 1958: Mike married his high school sweetheart, Sandra Bliss, in 1962. They moved back to the Dolan Homestead on Baker Road and raised three children and welcomed three grandchildren and one step-grandchild. Mike was an extreme Chicago Cub fan and an avid reader, having read the entire World Book Encyclopedia as well as Childcraft during his lifetime. He served on various farm boards and was a commentator at St. Mary's for 46 years. Mike died at age 71 in 2011 and is buried in St. Mary Cemetery.

CHARLOTTE DOLAN BORGOGNI: DHS class of 1962. In 1966, Charlotte graduated with a degree in education from Edgewood

College and married Vince Borgogni in St. Mary Church. She earned a master's degree in education from the University of Wisconsin at Whitewater in 1991. She was a kindergarten teacher and reading specialist in the Beloit public schools for 24 years, retiring in 2007. She and Vince still live in Beloit, where they raised three children and have six grandchildren.

FATHER JOSEPH A. DRISCOLL: After having baptized all 14 of us and providing spiritual security to our family throughout our polio crisis, Father Driscoll ended 27 years at St. Mary's when he was transferred in 1960 to St. Gall's Church in Elburn, Ill. He served there until he retired in 1967. He died in 1971 at age 78, just two weeks before his 50th anniversary of being a priest. He is buried in Mr. Olivet Cemetery in Aurora, Ill.

DR. CHARLES A. LEONARD: Dr. Leonard continued his private practice until his sudden death in 1978 at the age of 74. He was a founder of the Illinois chapter of the American Cancer Society and of Rockford Catholic Charities. He was survived by nine children and 24 grandchildren.

DR. GEORGE A. SAXTON: Seeing the swift decline of polio after the introduction of the Salk vaccine, Dr. Saxton changed his focus from curative to preventive medicine and continued teaching cardiopulmonary medicine at Illinois Research Hospital until 1959. He then spent a decade teaching in Uganda, with his wife Anne and their four children, until 1971. The rest of his career was spent practicing and teaching medicine, often with his wife. They received the Margaret Sanger Award in 1976 for their work in maternal and children's health care. Dr. Saxton was a founding member of the International Physicians for the Prevention of Nuclear War, now known as Physicians for Social Responsibility, which in 1985 won the Nobel Peace Prize. He died at age 82 in 2005.

DR. JANET WOLTER GRIP: Following the decline in polio cases, Dr. Grip moved down the street to Presbyterian Hospital, which later joined with St. Luke's Hospital and then resurrected Rush Medical School. She worked in what became the Section of Medical Oncology and eventually became a full professor of medicine. The last 25 years of her practice and teaching was focused on breast cancer. In 1996 Dr. Grip was the first occupant of the Brian Piccolo Chair of Breast Cancer Research. She was president of the Chicago Cancer Society and in 1999 became president of the medical staff of Rush University Medical Center. Dr. Grip retired in 2010 and continues to live a quiet life in Chicago.

JACK WALSH: DHS class of 1956. Jack worked a year following graduation to earn money to attend Northern Illinois University in DeKalb. He married Nancy Smith in 1960 and graduated with a degree in business management in 1961. He worked 30 years at Rockford Powertrain before retiring in 1994 to care for Nancy, who was afflicted with cancer. Following 40 years of marriage and raising two children, Nancy died in 2001 and is buried in St. Mary Cemetery. Jack married Lisa Greene in 2011 and now enjoys his two grandchildren, three step-grandchildren and four step-great grandchildren. He still calls Durand home although he has lived at Lake Summerset, about three miles northwest of Durand, since 1974. He has remained active at St. Mary's and Lake Summerset, serving on various boards and committees.

BOB HAGGERTY: DHS class of 1956. After graduating, Bob attended three colleges or universities before graduating from the University of Wisconsin at Whitewater in 1963. He married Ruth Johnson in 1967 and they raised a daughter. Bob loved having fun and was an avid Cubs fan. He worked in marketing and sales for several companies, including Colgate Palmolive. He enjoyed keeping in touch with his Durand buddies and made dozens of visits back to his hometown throughout his entire life. After being divorced and retiring,

Bob moved to Colorado to be near his daughter and grandchild. He died at age 70 in 2008 and his ashes are buried in St. Mary Cemetery.

NORM CHILTON: DHS class of 1956. Norm graduated in 1960 from the University of Wisconsin at Whitewater with a degree in business/accounting and economics. He joined the Wisconsin National Guard for two years and then joined his father's successful real-estate business in the Durand area. He lived in Rockford for many years, married Thomasetta (Tommy) Matuszewaki in 1969 and opened Chilton Real Estate in downtown Durand in 1970. Five years later he opened a second office at Lake Summerset. He and Tommy are the parents of two children. His son Eric has joined Norm in what is now the third generation of Chilton Real Estate.

DAVE MCCULLOUGH: DHS class of 1957. After graduating as valedictorian, Dave attended three universities but his heart was never in being a college student--he wanted to be a news photographer/cameraman in the television business. In 1959 he joined the staff of WREX in Rockford where he worked until 1963, when he accepted a news photography position at WCCO, the CBS station in Minneapolis. It was there, at one of the best local news television stations in the country, that Dave shot several documentaries overseas and won many national awards. In the 1980s he became the chief photographer for KTSP, the CBS affiliate in Phoenix. The station was sold in 1990, requiring that all employees undergo a physical, which revealed that Dave had lung cancer. He died 14 months later, in 1991. He and his wife Kate had one son, Gavin, who today is an anthropologist.

DAN MCCULLOUGH: DHS class of 1957. Twin brother of Dave, Dan graduated from Northern Illinois University with a bachelor's degree in education in 1961 and a master's degree in education in 1971. He taught middle school for 24 years before retiring from Kinnikinnick School in Roscoe, Ill. in 1985. Twelve years later Dan retired again, this time from working in the Winnebago County Regional Office of Education. He enjoys retirement—"I get up when I please, do what I please, go to bed when I please and repeat the process each day. It's been a full and mostly pleasant life, and the time has gone by almost as fast as the paychecks."

BEVERLY MEIER WALLER: DHS class of 1957: Two weeks after graduation, Bev married her high school sweetheart, Ken Waller. She was employed by the Durand School District for nearly 20 years, during which time she earned two associate degrees as a teachers' aide and in library/media technology. Bev has been a certified Illinois High School Association volleyball coach for 38 years. She and Ken had four children, including their oldest son Bob who was killed in 1985 in a go-cart race at Rockford Speedway. They still live in Durand and have seven grandchildren and two great grandchildren.

TOM SPELMAN: DHS class of 1957. After graduation, Tom joined the Air Force and then returned to Durand to help his dad manage the DX Service Station, of which he eventually became the owner. He was legendary for making people laugh. Once when he got into a bar scuffle with another patron, he tore the guy's shirt. "You have to buy me a new shirt," his adversary shouted. "I can't," Tom replied. "Why not?" asked the guy. "Because the Salvation Army store is closed," quipped Tom. He married Jill Linney in 1964 and they have three children, one granddaughter and five step-grandchildren. Tom died in 2011 and his wake at Daughenbaugh Funeral Home in Dakota drew hundreds of people, many standing in line for as long as four-and-a-half hours. His funeral was at St. Mary's and he is buried in St. Mary Cemetery.

ROGER SARVER: DHS class of 1955. Roger finished his schooling at Coyne Electrical Radio and Television in Chicago, a few blocks from Illinois Research Hospital, where he faithfully visited Dave and

Ed. In 1975 he married Bonnie Houghton. Together they have four children, nine grandchildren and two great grandchildren. Roger worked for 36 years at Barber-Coleman in Rockford in the Quality Control Department. He finished his career at Tri-Part Screw Products in suburban Rockford and retired in 2002. He continues to be active in Durand civic affairs and still enjoys playing golf.

DAN WALLER: DHS class of 1956. The president of Dave's senior class graduated in 1960 with a degree in electrical engineering from the University of Wisconsin at Madison. He spent two years in the Army and then joined the National Security Agency, where he worked until he retired in 1995. A life-long bachelor, he was active in St. Nicholas Catholic Church in Laurel, Md., until he died at age 67 in 2005. He is buried in St. Mary Cemetery.

PAUL G. NORSWORTHY: Durand's top school official retired in 1963 after 20 years of service as principal and superintendent. The school district named the school library in his honor and held a farewell open house for him and his wife Frieda that drew more than 500 people. The Norsworthys lived the next nine years on the west coast of Florida before he died at age 71 in 1972.

HARRY VALE: Durand was Mr. Vale's first teaching assignment and he remained for the next 16 years as the vocational agriculture teacher before teaching one year in Brodhead, Wis. He then left the teaching profession but not the hearts of Durand's students, parents and citizens. He became the manager of Lake Summerset for seven years and even squeezed in one term as Durand's mayor. He and his wife, Cres, one of Rose's tutors, raised three children while living in the home formerly owned by Paul and Frieda Norsworthy. The Vales then lived for the next 30 years on a farm in Albany, Wis. They have eight grandchildren, recently celebrated their 65th wedding anniversary and now live in Monroe, Wis.

KEN KRIENKE: Ken and his wife Bonnie lived in the cheese factory at Baker and Wheeler roads for several years before moving to Durand. If Ken got home early from work, he would still help Dad with the chores. He continued to work at the Miller Vault Company before accepting a position at Dean Foods in Rockford, where he worked for 27 years before retiring. He also owned and operated Krienke's Car Wash in Durand and Pecatonica. An Army veteran, he loved hunting and fishing with his sons. Ken died at age 85 in 2014, leaving four children, nine grandchildren and three great grandchildren. Bonnie still lives in Durand.

ART JOHNSON: A good friend of Dad's, Art continued to be active in Durand community affairs and served as vice president of Rockford's Central National Bank until his death at age 66 in 1966. He was survived by his wife, Caroline, two sons and 10 grandchildren. He is buried in St. Mary Cemetery.

WARD WALLER: The president of the Centennial celebration continued as one of Durand's two rural mail carriers until he retired in 1971. He remained active in the town's civic affairs and at St. Mary's, where he had been one of its first lay lectors and for many years its chairman of lectors. Like Dad, Ward also served a term as president of the school board. He and his wife Esther had five children, 12 grandchildren and three great grandchildren. He died at age 92 in 1999.

EVANS WHITMAN: After building the special additional room at our farm for Dave and Ed, Whitman completed other major projects in Durand, including the Durand State Bank and the Durand Medical Center, both in 1957, and the Durand Post Office in 1961. He died at age 56 in 1974.

ROCKFORD TOWNSHIP HOSPITAL: In 1956 the 198-bed

hospital and nursing home was given a new name—River Bluff Nursing Home. In 1957 the hospital section where our brothers and sisters were once cared for was closed. Today River Bluff is a 304-bed licensed skilled nursing facility.

ST. ANTHONY HOSPITAL: Now known as OSF St. Anthony's Medical Center, it has been serving patients for more than 100 years. It is now a 254-bed tertiary care facility on a 100-acre campus on the East Side of Rockford. It offers several medical services, including a trauma center, a neurological institute and a center for cancer care. It still is home to the St. Anthony College of Nursing, from which four of our sisters graduated.

"STRIKE IT RICH:" The popular but sometimes controversial game show aired on radio and television from June 1947 to January 1958. Over the years, many critics attacked the show because they thought it took advantage of poor people. Two attempts to revive it, in 1973 and 1978, failed.

ST. MARY CATHOLIC CHURCH: St. Mary and its mission church, St. Patrick in Irish Grove, have shown continued, steady growth over the years, mainly because of the development of Lake Summerset. After Father Driscoll left in 1960, eight more priests have shepherded our parish. In 1990 a new rectory was built and in 2004 a renovation of the church's interior was completed.

THE TOWN OF DURAND: The population of Durand has more than doubled since the mid-1950s to about 1,500. Some of the businesses, such as the Ford dealership, are still operating but with new owners. The town's oldest business, A. C. McCartney Farm Equipment, was founded in 1950 and is still doing business today in four locations, although its co-founder, Al McCartney, died at age 96 in 2015.

DURAND SCHOOL SYSTEM: New elementary classrooms

were opened in 1953 across the street from the high school and junior high school. In 1957 new high school classrooms were added to the elementary ones and the district closed the old high school-junior high school building. Expansion of the new school continued for the next 40 years. In 1977, the old school was demolished and replaced with a parking lot for teachers. Enrollment today is 581 pupils.

WINNEBAGO COUNTY 4-H FAIR: The 4-H Fair continued to be held on West State Street in Rockford until it merged with the Winnebago County Fair in 1974. The fair was then moved to the Pecatonica County Fairgrounds in Pecatonica, Ill., where it is still held today. The flavor of the fair has changed from rural to urban because of the decline in family livestock farms. Interest in homemaking and gardening has waned and given way to a wide range of new projects, including technology, global insight, career exploration and a variety of visual art offerings. Currently there is one 4-H Club in Durand, the New England Bells, which has 45 members.

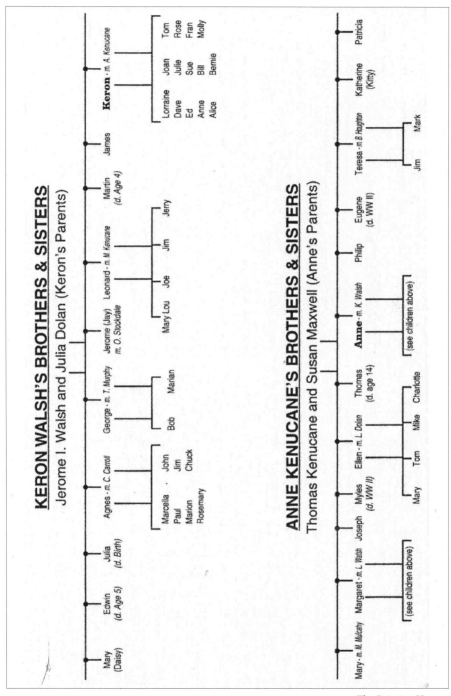

The Printing House.

183

ROSE'S EPILOGUE

I am the plucky little girl in the polio pictures. At least the captions under the pictures say that's me. I do not remember having polio. I got it a few days after my fifth birthday. Today kids start school when they are five years old. The Durand School District did not have kindergarten in 1955. Going to kindergarten would have been a lot more fun than going to the hospital. That's what I did during the first week of the school year in September 1955.

I do not remember the day I got sick. I think I remember the waiting room in Dr. Leonard's office; it was dark, with a lamp on. Maybe that's why to this day I feel anxious when sitting in a doctor's waiting room.

I was at Rockford Township Hospital for about a week. I think I recall being in a bed and hearing a car horn honking in the distance. It kept honking and honking and honking, like it was stuck. That must have been at Township Hospital, where my room was on the first floor.

I recall a few more things seen from St. Anthony's Hospital, where I was for more than two months. There was a swinging door to the pediatric unit that was partly glass. I probably had never seen a swinging door before.

The smell of hot moist wool is a very clear memory. This must have been from the hot packs. They were part of the Sister Kenny treatment method for polio. The hot packs were used, literally, to warm-up weakened muscles prior to vigorous physical therapy (PT) sessions of stretching, range-of-motion and strengthening exercises. I do not remember having them applied to my arms and legs — just the smell. It's not a good or bad smell, but a very distinctive one. When I smell it now, which is seldom, it makes me think of hospitals.

I remember the yellow chenille bathrobe that Roy Rogers and Dale Evans sent to me. They did that after seeing my picture, with a Dale Evans book behind me, in their newspaper. The soft robe had many colors on the pockets. I am wearing it in the picture with Ed at St. Anthony's Hospital. Maybe I just remember hearing about this gift and seeing it in the photos.

I also think that I remember seeing Dad carry Molly down the hall when she was admitted to treat her eye injury in early November 1955. The nurse shut the door to my room so Molly wouldn't see me and get upset. Even so, I saw them. Molly had her arms around Dad's neck. He was looking the other way from my room.

I was at St. Anthony's mostly for therapy until the day before Thanksgiving. I had recovered from polio, but some of my muscles never would. My right leg has been weak ever since. I have always walked with a limp. I came home from the hospital wearing a corset because of my weak abdominal muscles.

Luckily, my other muscles were all right. I could walk without wearing heavy leg braces like other "polio kids." I had never needed to be in an iron lung like my two big brothers. I must have felt very happy while eating turkey and my favorite raisin stuffing at home with my family.

I was home but still needed a lot of PT. In addition to twice-a-week trips to St. Anthony's therapy department, there were twice-a-day exercise sessions at home. Lorraine and Alice were in charge of these. I do not recall what the exercises were or the 30-minute trips to St. Anthony's. I do remember the names of my physical therapist, Miss Janet Cook, and her aide, Gussie. Mom used to tell me that Gussie made me giggle.

The one thing that I do remember about going to PT is always stopping for a treat on the way home! I couldn't wait till Mom pulled into Sparky's, a small grocery store on the edge of Rockford. This was big stuff for a little Walsh kid. Going somewhere alone with Mom and getting a treat from somewhere other than Bentley's grocery store in Durand made an everlasting impression on my five-year-old brain. No matter how busy Mom was, she would let me go into the store and browse even though she knew I would pick one of my favorites: a Bun candy bar or a Twinkie.

I am not sure where I slept after I had polio. It was not with Anne and Alice where I was sleeping when I woke up so sick that September. Mom wrote in a December 1955 letter to Dave that "We bought Rosie a new bed. It is really a baby bed, but it is her very own. She can have a little privacy this way. It is maple in color, and has a big pink lamb decal on one end." I vaguely recall sleeping in it in the dining room but I am not sure when that was.

The events of 1956-57 blur together for me. Only now, as I look back, can I sort my recollections of them into the right year. I recall wearing a new dress with a red belt. There is nothing blurry about my memory of that red belt; it was wide and shiny patent leather. It must have fascinated me. For some reason I associate that belt with being at Dave's high school graduation in Chicago. The newspaper articles stated that all of us were there in June 1956. I am sure that Mom had each of us dressed in our Sunday best.

I think I was in the kitchen shortly after Mom got the call that Ed had died in August 1956. She was sitting at the long kitchen table by the phone. Dad was standing in the porch door, wiping tears from his eyes. It was very quiet. It was probably the only time I saw him cry.

I remember one of the wakes, maybe both, but they blend together. There were a lot of people getting our house ready for the wake. I recall standing in a doorway, watching someone in the driveway carrying furniture, maybe a chair.

The casket was placed along the west wall of the small living room. It was in front of a window. There were two big candles, in tall candle holders, at each end of it.

During one of the wakes, probably Dave's in 1957, I lay across

Dad and Mom's laps as they greeted the never-ending line of mourners. They sat on the green davenport, along the north wall, about five or six feet from the casket. The line of cars parked along Baker Road stretched all the way up the hill.

I do not remember being at the funerals, or ever hearing anyone mention them.

Shortly after Ed's funeral I turned six; it was time for first grade. It was my turn to join my other brothers and sisters on the school bus. I vaguely recall being in Mrs. Geist's first grade classroom. I hadn't been there long when my doctor decided it was more important that I continue going to my outpatient PT.

Aunt Margaret, a teacher, was chosen to be my home tutor. She came for about an hour and a half each morning. I sat in a school desk for my lessons in "readin' and writin' and 'rithmetic." Sometimes my very favorite doll, Mary Anne, would sit with me at my desk. Aunt Margaret and Mom taught me the words to a poem about a doll named Mary Anne, just like mine. It was called "The Mortifying Mistake."

Not going to school also gave me time for doing my twice-daily exercises at home, during the "quiet" school day. Lorraine must have done them with me when Mom was visiting "the boys" in the hospital. I was constantly reminded to keep my weak right foot "in" when I walked. I can still hear our hired man saying, "Keep your foot in" as he watched me walk. He meant well, but the reminders probably didn't help; my foot would forever be weak and turn out.

Even worse, my weak abdominal muscles weren't doing a good job of helping to keep my spine straight. Neither was the tight corset that I wore all of the time. It felt cold on my skin on winter mornings. Sometimes I would have to go see Lloyd, an orthoptist (brace maker), to adjust my corset. His shop was in downtown Rockford on a busy street. He was a short man with dark wavy hair. His exam rooms had curtains, not doors. That's all I remember about being there.

The best part of going to Lloyd's was getting to stop at Pete's afterwards! Pete's Snack Bar was across the street and had better treats than Sparky's. I think we would get lunch, or maybe just ice cream. What I really remember are the red bar stools at the soda fountain. I could make the stool spin around until I got a little dizzy. No wonder I told Mom that I thought Pete's was "snazzy"— spinning was fun!

I would go see Dr. Leonard for regular check-ups. The multi-story building where his office was had a big heavy revolving entrance door. Fran and Molly and I would giggle as we walked "around" the door, and run to get out of it when we got inside. Then we would ride the elevator up to his office.

Another way that my weak abdominals affected me was that I had a weak cough. I remember whenever I had a bad cold, Mom would have me lie across her bed on my tummy, with my head and shoulders hanging over the edge. She would ask me to cough, and when I did she would tap on my back, over my lungs. She was doing her version of postural drainage. The tapping helped to loosen the phlegm, since I could not cough hard enough to get it up. I think she taught some of the big girls how to do the tapping. Two other memories of having a cold: the hot water vaporizer next to the bed and the awful taste of the cough syrup.

Another memory from that time is being in Dave's Room with him. He liked popular songs and had a lot of 45 rpm records. One thing I could do to help was to play the records for him. He had a small record player on a table by the right side of his bed. I could stack several records at once and they would drop down, one at a time, to be played. I played "Blueberry Hill" by Fats Domino a lot. It must have been one of Dave's favorites. I also remember his long bathtub, and watching him being transferred into it.

Sometime in early 1957, Dr. Leonard told Mom that he was concerned about my spine. He was quite sure that my spinal curve (scoliosis) was getting worse. He referred us to a specialist, Dr. Donald Lyddon, an orthopedic surgeon.

Dr. Lyddon's office was close to St. Anthony Hospital — I think on Charles Street. It was very different from Dr. Leonard's dark office. The big open waiting area in this newer building had a lot of light and maybe even several windows. I remember that Dr. Lyddon was tall.

On one of my trips to Rockford in December, we went to a store, maybe a Goldblatt's, with a mechanical Christmas display in the big front window. It mesmerized me and I did not want to stop watching it. I don't remember what was in the display, only that it moved, and I had never seen anything like it. It was magical.

It probably didn't take Dr. Lyddon long to decide that I needed major spine surgery. My spine was steadily curving to the right side, due to my very weak abdominal muscles. Mom told me later that he explained it as "like trying to hold a flexible pole straight with no guy wires."

The first step in this long "straightening" process was for me to be fitted with a brace at Lloyd's shop. The metal and leather Milwaukee Brace looked like a contraption from the Middle Ages. It had a leather "girdle" that fit around my pelvis. The girdle had three long metal rods attached to it — two in the back and one in the front. The two in the back attached at the top to the padded rest for the back of my head. The front metal piece attached to the leather-padded "ledge" for my chin.

It had a front piece and a back piece. The back half went on first, when I was lying on my side, and the front half, with the chin pad, went on last, when I was on my back. I think there were side buckles on the girdle piece. There were screws on each side of the neck to hold it in place.

When the brace was finished, and fitted properly, I wore it for about a month before the surgery. This was in hopes that my spine would straighten somewhat before it was fused. I would then wear it for 24 hours a day during my six months of postoperative bed rest. An orthopedic surgeon in Milwaukee invented the brace to immobilize his spinal fusion patients.

The surgery was like a remodeling project. It involved reinforcing several of my vertebrae with bone pieces from my shin (tibia) bone. Because I was so young, it was a two-part surgery. The first part, during which five vertebrae and one leg were worked on, was done on April 22, 1957. Two or three weeks later, I was back in the operating room for Round Two, when four or five other vertebrae, with bone from my other leg, were done. Luckily, I don't remember much about either one.

Some things I do remember are a BIG light above me and people in surgical gowns looking down at me. I must have been on the operating table, with the bright light over it. The people must have been the operating-room team; maybe Dr. Lydden was one of them. Also I remember the strong smell of ether, or whatever anesthesia was used for six-year-olds in 1957.

I think I also remember going fast as I was being pushed through the hall on the way to the operating room. I was probably very scared. I do not remember being in the brace when I woke up, but I must have been.

Mom told me often that I was very ill after these surgeries. I vomited a lot, which was probably hard to do with the brace under my chin. Mom told me that it was Demerol, a pain medication that made me sick. She would say, "Don't ever let anyone give you Demerol again."

I only remember one nurse. Her name was Mary Jo. She probably helped me often when I was sick. Her uniform was a shiny pink jumper with a white blouse.

I remember that one of my get-well gifts was the cutest stuffed animal I had ever seen — a very soft orange and yellow Easter rabbit. I loved it and think I remember playing with it in the hospital. I still have some of my many get-well cards. One of my favorite had a white "flocked" cat on the front that was fun to touch; the white cat had blue rhinestone eyes.

I have been told that I was in bed with the brace on until November. I do not recall being in bed in Dave's Room, but I must have been for a couple of months. I do remember sleeping in the dining room so that I could be closer to Mom and Dad. I have a vague memory of seeing Dave's night nurse, Mrs. Fowler, walking through the dining room and into Dave's Room to help him.

I wish that I remembered more about my unique first communion in July 1957, a few weeks after Dave was taken back to Chicago. Even though I was unable to be at St. Mary's to receive communion with my catechism classmates, I had a very special ceremony at home with my friends. Aunt Margaret, my teacher, was there and wrote:

"…The procession of altar boys and First Communicants preceded the priest into the room where Rose Ellen lay on her bed….They were followed by her Father and Mother, her brothers and sisters, an aunt who lived nearby and her teacher. Rose Ellen was dressed in a pure white dress, with a wreath and veil on her head. On her feet were white slippers which had never touched the floor."

The only clear memory I have of this big event happened the day before. That is when Father Driscoll came to hear my first confession. He seemed huge as he sat by the head of my bed. I was flat on my back when he leaned his bald head close, so he could hear me. His big green (or were they blue?) eyes looked way too big. I remember being very scared. I was probably glad when it was over.

There was a big thunderstorm that Monday morning of July 8th. I remember that the sky got very dark. I was looking out the window towards the barn during the storm. Most of my memories of my first communion are probably from looking at the pictures taken that day.

Dave died two months later, during my six months of bed rest. I must have had my brace on when I recall lying on Mom and Dad's laps during Dave's wake.

Although I recall little about the extensive surgery I had and my long recuperation time, I always had a reminder with me — the scars on both of my shins. I called them "my zippers," because all along both sides of the six-inch incision scars were little dots. The dots were scars from each stitch; there were little dots about every ½ inch. I knew I had a much longer zipper down my back, but I could never see it.

I continued to be "home-schooled" for most of second grade during the 1957-58 school year. I may have gone to school in the spring; I am not sure. I remember Aunt Margaret teaching me. I was lying on my tummy, on my bed mattress, which was on the kitchen table. I can't imagine lying on my tummy in the brace, but being on the table for "school" is a clear memory.

I recovered from the surgery, was able to gradually shed the cumbersome brace and finally started going to school in the fall of 1958. Mrs. Panoske was my third grade teacher. I don't remember anyone at school ever mentioning about me having had polio. I tried everything the other kids did, even in gym class. I hated what I called the "tumbling unit," and I'm not sure I ever mastered the skills needed to turn a somersault, but I sure did try! I also remember trying over and over to climb up a long, rough, scratchy rope suspended from the ceiling. I am glad that rope-climbing is not critical for success because I flunked that skill.

In fifth grade I started learning how to play the clarinet. Music lessons were much more my style than PE. I was in band until I graduated from high school.

I joined 4-H when I was 10, but was only in it for one year. I made a pink and white skirt with an elastic waistband. I had to bring three muffins to the fair for my baking project. I don't ever recall wearing the skirt or baking any more muffins, but I used my sewing and baking skills forever.

I learned another very important life-long skill when I was 10 years old. I learned how to ride a bike. This was not easy to do, since we only had one bike — an orange, three-speed boy's bike. It was Bill's pride and joy. It was way too big for me but that didn't matter, I was bound and determined to ride it. So I rode up and down the road to Aunt Daisy's driveway and back to our driveway. The problem was

I had no idea of how to turn the bike around. Instead, I would slow down, start tipping to one side and jump off (hopefully) before the shiny bike crashed to the ground.

These were things I learned I could do, but one thing I could not do was to stop my spine from curving as I grew. By seventh grade in 1962, it was obvious that the surgery to stabilize my spine had not been successful. It curved gradually as I went about my "pre-teen, junior-high business," talking on the phone, listening to music on the radio and dancing to records during lunch hour.

So it was back to another doctor's waiting room, to another Milwaukee Brace and to another operating table for 12-year-old me. This time my surgeon, Dr. Walter Blount, was in Milwaukee; he had invented the brace. I am not exactly sure how I ended up in his office, but Dr. Leonard referred me to him. His waiting room was small. It was a long narrow room with windows at one end. The receptionist sat at a desk behind a glass sliding window.

We would find out later that Dr. Blount was held in high esteem by his colleagues in the world of spinal surgery. Even though he was world-renowned, he had great compassion for his patients. He knew of my family's background and arranged for a reduced rate on the cost of my surgery, telling Dad and Mom that he believed in "cheaper by the dozen."

The first time he saw me he had no doubt that I needed surgery and a new Milwaukee Brace. He would have preferred that I have my brace made and fitted in Milwaukee, but referred us to an orthoptist (brace maker) in Rockford. His name was Lothar Grade. I think he was from Germany.

I wore the brace for about a month before the surgery. The night before I went to the hospital, Mom told me there was a 50-50 chance that I would not be able to walk after the surgery. Even worse, there was a slim chance that I would not survive. We were sitting on the green couch in the living room. We cried together, said some prayers and went to bed.

Our prayers were answered two days later on Aug. 1, 1963. I was able to move my legs in the recovery room, which was an excellent sign that I would be able to walk. I had come through the long seven-hour operation with the crucial nerves of my spinal cord still intact.

During the surgery, Dr. Blount's skilled hands cut bone from my ribs and used it to fuse seven or eight of my thoracic vertebrae. Impressive as that is, it is even more, knowing that he had significant hand and arm tremors. I am not certain that he had Parkinson's disease, but he certainly had strong tremors. When he saw me in his office he would hold his hands together to reduce the shakiness. His young partner, Dr. Zuege, probably assisted him with complex surgeries.

Unlike my earlier hospital stays, I remember a lot about this one. The day of surgery is fuzzy — I remember the anesthesiologist putting the mask over my nose and mouth and asking me to count, and then someone far away was asking me to move my legs and wiggle my toes. It seemed like a minute later that I heard that, but it must have been at least seven hours later.

I recall being wheeled back into my room, and then the next time I "came to" was two days later.

I am sure I woke up at times the day after surgery but I have no recollection of that day. I think my big sister Anne was there with Mom when I was fully awake. I was surprised when she told me what day it was.

My room was on the sixth floor, on the south side of the building at 700 W. Wisconsin Ave. The Marquette University campus was nearby, a dorm was across the street. From my window I could see the three botanical garden domes being built at Mitchell Park on 35th Street.

I remember that there were several very good-looking interns and residents who made rounds with Dr. Blount. The residents would check on me much more often than my doctor did. My favorite was Dr.

Howard. I had quite the pre-teen crush on him!

Like other pre-teens I often listened to the Top 40 hits on A.M. radio. The Four Seasons were very popular and I heard their hit song, "Sherry," over and over again. Another song I recall hearing was "Big John" by Tennessee Ernie Ford. My roommate and I used to sing along to the songs. She was from Wichita Falls, Tex.

I looked forward to going to the playroom on the sixth floor. The staff would push my bed down the hall and into the big room where there were lots of other kids. Two occupational therapists set up craft activities and games to play. I still remember making a 10-inch ball by folding several small paper circles around a triangle. I hung it in my room.

Some days I would have to go to physical therapy instead of to the playroom. A couple of weeks after my surgery, the physical therapist put me on a tilt table and tilted me up at a 45-degree angle. Each time I was on it, I was tilted a little more upright. I had many safety belts around me. The purpose was for me to bear weight on my legs without having to stand up.

Dr. Blount was there the first time I was tilted up to a full 90-degree position. He wanted to see my response to "standing" and was pleased by what he saw. He had several doctors from Australia with him that day.

Mom visited me often. She often took the train from Durand. Her cousin Margaret Carroll lived in Milwaukee, but Mom did not stay at her apartment. Margaret did not have a car, so they would meet for lunch at a buffet place close to the hospital. Mom stayed at the YMCA on Wisconsin Avenue.

During my month in the hospital there was BIG news from home. Bill showed the grand champion steer at the 4-H fair. That was a thrill for our family, especially for Dad. He was so proud of his Angus herd, and to have one of his steers judged to be the "best in show" was a great honor. Two days later the steer was sold for a record-breaking price per pound. I was sorry to miss out on all this excitement.

There was also excitement about Joan's wedding plans. Jerry Didier had proposed to her in the spring of 1963 and they chose Oct. 5 for their big day. Mom updated me on "the latest" about the plans during her visits. I was glad to hear the reception would be at our house. I would miss the wedding at our church but not the party-after.

When it was time to go home from the hospital, the question was, "How would I get there?" The surprising answer was, in a hearse! Why? In 1963 we no longer had our station wagon, so Dad decided to ask if he could borrow Durand's only emergency vehicle/ambulance. That vehicle was actually Chapin's hearse! Mr. and Mrs. Chapin owned a furniture store, which was also the town's only funeral home. They loaned the hearse to Dad for a day, with no questions asked.

The big day came and I was loaded into the back of the hearse for the two-hour ride home from Milwaukee. I must have been on some kind of stretcher. Dad and Mom let Fran and Molly come along with them. They were fun company on the way home. They would pull the maroon velvet drapes open and wave to people.

Dad stopped for gas in Clinton, Wis. and people were staring at the hearse. I asked Fran to open the curtain on the back window. Then I held my foot up to the window and began waving with it. The people really stared at that! We were all, Mom included, laughing at people's reactions.

It was great to be home again. My 13th birthday (Aug. 30) was the next day. A few days later Mom invited some of my classmates to a birthday party for me. They had just started back to school, for our eighth-grade year. I would have been in Mr. Mulera's home room. Instead, I was home in Dave's Room with my tutor, Mrs. Vale

She came every day at 1 p.m. for two hours. She will always be a part of my memories of Nov. 22, 1963, the day President Kennedy was assassinated. Mrs. Vale arrived a few minutes after Aunt Daisy had called to tell Mom the awful news from Dallas. She stayed a few minutes and knew that neither one of us would be able to focus on my lessons, so she went home.

For the next three days our family watched the news coverage of the events in D.C. and Dallas. We had one television in our small living room. When I wanted to watch TV, my hospital bed was pushed into the dining room. I would be rolled onto my left side to watch from the dining room. The other shows I remember watching were Red Skelton, The Fugitive, Ben Casey, Gunsmoke and Ed Sullivan.

In December 1963, the doctor said I could start standing for brief periods two to three times a day. I was able to help decorate the Christmas tree for a few minutes. That year we had two trees, our traditional evergreen one in the living room and a white flocked tree in Dave's Room. Mom used blue ornaments and blue lights on the white tree. I remember lying in bed thinking how beautiful it was.

After three months, Mom could give me sponge baths with the brace off; putting it back on was quite a job. The front and back parts were connected by sliding metal pieces on each side of my neck. Once the two parts were slid into place, they were held with small screws. Dad sputtered his favorite word—"Golly"—many times while tightening those little screws. It was kind of scary to have a screwdriver that close to my neck.

By spring I was "up-and-around" with the brace on. I remember that Mom wanted me to go to my eighth-grade graduation. She bought me a cute lavender gingham dress with flowers embroidered on it for the occasion. It was hard to find "teen-age" clothes to fit over the bulky brace.

I liked the dress but did not like the idea of walking across the stage in the old high school building. I was still being tutored at home and had never been at school with my brace on. I was very self-conscious about being seen in public. The day came for the graduation; Mom helped me get ready, but then I refused to get in the car. I was standing in the front yard when the car left for town and I watched it go up the road. Very little was said when they came home from the graduation. It was probably silly of me to be so stubborn.

I must have gone "out-and-about" during the summer because in August 1964 I felt comfortable enough to start high school wearing the Milwaukee Brace. School shopping had not been very fun that year. In the 1960s kids did not wear T-shirts to school and girls could not wear pants. There were not many fun blouses or dresses that worked with the brace. We did find a fun dress with a high waist. The top was polka-dot and the skirt was striped.

The first day went well, until the last hour. That's when I was broadsided in the hallway. I was walking out of the library, making a left turn, when a big guy happened to be walking past the library door and BOOM — we collided. I literally did not know what hit me. Luckily, I was not hurt, except for my pride. I quickly picked up my things that went sprawling everywhere. The guy helped me up from the floor, said he was sorry, and we kept walking. I don't remember other people in the hallway.

I was so embarrassed that I am not sure I told anyone for awhile. There was little, if any, mention of my brace at school. I had very few accommodations because of my condition. The school desks were very uncomfortable for me with the brace on, so there was a small table for me in each of my classrooms.

After a couple of months I was able to be "brace-free" for half of the school day. This was easier said than done, since no one at school knew how to help with the brace. My big brother, Bernie, a senior in high school, was the solution. During lunch hour Bernie drove me the few blocks to Aunt Margaret's home, where he took my brace off. I think that we then put the brace in a pillowcase, carried it to the car and went back to school. The whole process probably took about 20 to 30 minutes. Not many brothers would have wanted to leave their friends at such an important social time in the school day. I am not sure how long we did this routine; I would guess for two to three months.

Christmas 1964 was especially busy because three days later I was Julie's bridesmaid. Frank Willkom and Julie were married on Dec. 28, her 23rd birthday. I wore a long aqua-satin dress with a high back. During the wedding I had my brace off, but had to put it on right afterwards. At the reception in South Beloit, I was again brace-free.

In February 1965, my freshman year was interrupted by a trip back to Milwaukee Children's Hospital. Dr. Blount was, overall, pleased with how I had healed from the fusion but was concerned about one area in my mid-back. During my check-ups he would closely study my X-rays. In early January 1965, he had told us that he would have to repair the fusion on one vertebra (T11) and that I would have to spend more time in the Milwaukee Brace.

Dr. Blount also recommended a new type of surgery for my weak abdominal muscles. It was a fascia (tissue) transplant into my abdomen, in hopes that it would support my muscles. Mom and Dad were hesitant, but they trusted Dr. Blount so they agreed to the surgery.

But first I had important business to tend to — a school dance. In mid-February I went to the Cupid's Ball, the annual FHA valentine dance. Mom altered a petty pink dress so that it had a high back. I asked Jim Thomas to be my date and that's all I remember about it. Sandy Shippy had a freshman party after the dance. We played a karaoke-type game by "lip-synching" to records. My song to "sing" was "Downtown," by Petula Clark; that was fun.

A few days after the dance I had the repair surgery. Two or three weeks later I had the abdominal surgery. I really do not remember anything about either one, probably because they were relatively minor. I don't know how long I was in the hospital. It must have been awhile because I remember working with Mrs. G., a hospital teacher; I had to write reports for her.

Mom would bring me pretty yellow daffodils when she came to visit. I also remember that our cousin, Jo Ellen Walsh (Jack Walsh's youngest sister), came to visit me often. She was a Marquette University nursing student so her dorm was very close to the hospital.

I don't think that I returned to school that spring because in the summer I was tutored for algebra. My tutor was none other than Durand's school superintendent, Mr. Gordon Grande. I have no idea how he was selected to come to our home two or three mornings a week. I think the hospital teacher had helped me keep up in English and History only.

The abdominal surgery was not successful; the implanted fascia tissue did not "transplant" well. My spinal fusion repair surgery was very successful. I was gradually "weaned" from wearing the bulky brace. I did have to wear it to Sue and John Cocoma's wedding on July 31, 1965, but a month later I started my sophomore year "brace-free." For the first three months, I took a "doctor-ordered" rest time during the school day. After lunch I went to the nurse's room and would lie down on a cot for 30 minutes.

Luckily, that was the end of my Milwaukee Brace days; the surgeries for my polio residuals were over. Ten years after I had polio, I probably hoped that I was done with it. I didn't have to work hard to forget about it. My polio "stuff" was rarely mentioned, especially at school. I probably wore some type of corset, but don't remember it. I still limped but was not aware that I did. I had a lift on my right shoe, but it blended in and was hard to see.

I remember the day in junior English class that we played a "Who am I thinking of?" game. We each had to describe a classmate, using as few words as possible, and classmates guessed who the person was. A new girl in Durand used a clue of "this person has a stiff back." Several kids immediately guessed that it was me. I was surprised and puzzled because I had no idea that my back looked stiff.

I also remember my first year (1968-69) on the campus at Western Illinois University in Macomb, where I walked everywhere. It made me feel uncomfortable when others would ask me, "What happened to your leg?" or "How did you hurt your foot?" I am not sure why I didn't just answer, "I had polio," but I never did. I would make up different reasons for my limp.

I also shopped for clothes that covered up the curve in my back. Years later I discovered this kind of "cover-up" was very common for polio survivors. As a group, we tend to know no limitations. I did not feel I had any limits to what I could do. My childhood career dream was to be like Barbara Walters. I wanted to report from the United Nations building in New York City. I was disappointed that WIU only offered a minor in journalism. I took every journalism course offered while completing my history degree.

During my senior year at WIU, I totally "switched gears" when I realized that I would rather work with children. I already knew teaching was not for me. While considering other options, my happy hours in the playroom at Milwaukee Children's Hospital came to mind. I decided I wanted to be an occupational therapist.

I graduated with my Bachelor of Arts degree in 1972. I sought out OT programs designed for those with college degrees. In August 1973, I moved to Pennsylvania. My tiny studio apartment was one block from the University of Pennsylvania. I was totally unaware I had enrolled in an Ivy League school.

My OT training took me to Johns Hopkins Hospital in Baltimore and to a psychiatric hospital in Chicago, which was two blocks from where Dave and Ed had been patients. My job search took me to Iowa City, where I started my first OT job at the University of Iowa in February 1975. Twenty years after the polio, I was no longer the sick little girl in the newspapers. I was just Rose, an independent young woman ready for her next adventure — a real job.

Forty-one years and a "wonderful-life" later, I am still in Iowa City.

NOTES

Sources who are clearly identified in the text or are the authors are not included in these notes.

CHAPTER 1: "I See Snakes"

7—**"Temperatures reached…unheard of for Northern Illinois."** Weather records provided by Eric Sorensen, chief meteorologist, WREX-TV, Rockford, Ill.

7-8—**"Our oldest brothers…and take the 12-foot plunge from the rope into the water."** Julia Walsh Willkom memoirs, 2006.

8—**"Shortly after installing the plank…but the mud had sucked them up."** Notes from Bill Walsh, October 2006.

8—**"Often the boys camped…Jack Walsh remembered."** Jack Walsh interview, Aug. 8, 2011.

8-9—**"Few ever toppled Ed…Bob Haggerty rarely beat Ed."** Bill Haggerty interview, Feb. 2, 2013.

9—**"Down the creek…blood suckers off our feet."** Julia Walsh Willkom memoirs, 2006.

10—**"Joe Walsh…was stricken…working in the haymow."** Notes from Anne Walsh Colby, September 2006.

10—**"Alice and Anne…we prepared our suitcases for a week."** Notes from Anne Walsh Colby, September 2006.

10—**"Marian Walsh called our house…was more than the entire family could bear—so sudden, so beyond help."** Anne Walsh in a letter in the early 1980s to her children and grandchildren describing the tragic polio years.

10—**"…our older sisters…who their new teachers and classmates would be."** Notes from Anne Walsh Colby, September 2006.

11—**"No longer did they attend Dolan School…teachers boarded next door with Aunt Daisy."** Interview with Tom Dolan, May 7, 2015.

11—**"But in 1952 the Durand school district…began busing all the rural children to Durand's schools."** *Changing Ways, a history of the people in the Durand School District.*

11—**"The night before the opening day of school…for fear of getting sick and missing the first day of school."** Interview with Charlotte Dolan Borgogni, June 29, 2011.

11—**"The next morning, on Thursday, Sept 1, the big day arrived."** There is a conflict in the date of the first day of school. Anne Walsh, in her letter to her children and grandchildren in the mid-80s, says the first day of school, when Rose was taken to the doctor with polio, was Sept. 3. But it couldn't have been because Sept. 3 was a Saturday. The 1955 school yearbook included a school calendar and said school opened on Aug. 31, a Wednesday. Elsewhere, the yearbook said classes began Sept. 1, a Thursday. It's likely that school opened on Aug. 31, but for teachers only, and students attended their first classes on Thursday, Sept. 1.

11—**"Everyone was scampering…Rose woke up and announced to Alice: 'I see snakes." Notes from Alice Walsh Kraiss, 2004, 2011.

CHAPTER 2: Growing Up

13-14—"The cost of living in 1955...Eisenhower increased the minimum wage to $1.00 an hour." *Remember When—1955.*

14—"The first television station...an NBC affiliate on May 3, 1953." *Durand's Marvelous Merchants,* Chapter 6, Page 99.

14—"Two years later...'The Ed Sullivan Show.'" *Remember When—1955.*

14—"Dave and Jack loved to race...each in their '48 green Chevys." Interviews with Jack Walsh, Aug. 8, 2011, and with Tom Dolan, May 7, 2015.

14-15—"Yale Bridge Road...an extra week would be added to the penalty." Interview with Jack Walsh, April 1, 2008.

15-17—"Dave loved to drive Dad's '52 Chevy...Jack said he didn't remember." Interview with Jack Walsh, April 1, 2011.

17—"Like the boys in town...Rockford, Beloit or Freeport." Interview with Tom Dolan, May 7, 2015.

17—"Huge crowds, many in parked cars...in Northern Illinois and Southern Wisconsin." *Durand's Marvelous Merchants.*

17—"In 1939...Dad was their manager." *Durand Gazette,* May 1939.

18—"Another sport the boys enjoyed...in the haymow." Interview with Jim Walsh, Jan. 10, 2012.

18—"Dad insisted...full-time help on the farm." Julia Walsh Willkom memoirs, 2006.

18—"The boys favorite activity was hunting...they didn't taste too bad, Mike said." Interview with Mike Dolan, July 5, 2011.

18—"One evening Norm Chilton was bowling...a bullet was lodged in the bird's head." Interview with Norm Chilton, April 20, 2013.

CHAPTER 3: Faith and Fun

21—"Father Joseph A. Driscoll recruited...towering over the other three." Interview with Jack Walsh, April 1, 2008.

21—"After attending the visitation...the image stuck forever in Florence's mind." Interview with Florence Walsh.

21-22—"One Saturday night Jack, Bob and Dave...St. Mary's didn't need a public address system until he left in 1960." Interview with Jack Walsh, Aug. 8, 2011.

22—"Father Driscoll, who arrived at St. Mary's in 1933...Father usually bowled with us." *The Rockford Morning Star,* June 18, 1971.

22—"Father also attended Cubs games...he loved to talk, Bill said." Interview with town barber Bill Steward, May 31, 2012.

23—"As much as Father loved bowling, he loved even more being umpire...anything, Bob said, to avoid classwork." Interview with Jack Walsh, April 1, 2008.

23—"Everyone looked forward to recess…but secretly were delighted." *Durand's Marvelous Merchants*, Chapter 6, Page 100.

23—"Every August Dad took all of us…to Trask Bridge Picnic…largest country picnic." Julia Walsh Willkom memoirs, 2006.

23-24—"Located on farmland…fly casting, hog calling and husband calling." *The Durand Gazette, Aug. 21, 1930.*

24—"Dave and Ed and the Dolan boys…raised and showed Shorthorn cattle." Interview with Tom Dolan, May 7, 2015.

24-25—"During monthly 4-H club meetings…scaring people until being captured." Julia Walsh Willkom memoirs, 2006.

25-26—"Showmanship ability was essential…awarded him the top Showmanship Prize." Interview with Mike Dolan, July 5, 2011.

26—"It was so typical of Dave's personality…but never caused trouble." Interviews with Mike Dolan, July 5, 2011, and Jim Walsh, Jan. 10, 2012.

26—"Ed was much more reserved and studious…were neck-and-neck when they started their junior year in September 1955." Interviews with Mike Dolan, July 5, 2011, Jim Walsh, Jan. 10, 2012, Dan McCullough, May 31, 2012 and notes from Bev Meier Waller, 2002.

26—"Arm wrestling wasn't the only activity…very quiet with no more teasing." Bernie Walsh notes, August 2015.

26—"Ed never mentioned any plans for the future." Interview with Mike Dolan, July 5, 2011.

27—"Maybe Ed would be a carpenter…shadow box for our nativity set." Julie Walsh Willkom, summer 2015.

27—"As part of FFA classes…stools on the corners for the littlest ones." Interview with Harry Vale, Nov. 16, 2011.

27-28—"4-H was an important summertime activity…continued working at Alden's." Notes from Lorraine Walsh Vormezeele, October 2006, and Anne Walsh Colby, September 2006.

28-29—"Our 4-H leaders helped us…Delphiniums and phlox were her favorites." Notes from all the older sisters.

29-30—"One summer for the fair…Julie followed Mom's lead…'but I was so glad to get home.'" Julia Walsh Willkom memoirs, 2006.

CHAPTER 4: Brown Paper Bag #1

35-36—"The bus, driven as usual…change into their new Montgomery Ward's clothes." Notes from Lorraine Walsh Vormezeele, October 2006, and Anne Walsh Colby, September 2006, and Julia Walsh Willkom memoirs, 2006

36—"Joan and Julie were starting…seemed to have more than just the flu." Julia

Walsh Willkom memoirs, 2006.

36-37—"Shortly after the bus left, Mom raced to the barn…Mom retrieved it quickly." Anne Walsh's letter to her children and grandchildren.

37—"Mom didn't wait long to her youngest sister…we'll be OK." Notes from Pat Kenucane.

37—"Lorraine found out…your sister Rose has polio." Notes from Lorraine Walsh Vormezeele, October 2006.

37—"Dave was helping…I hope I never get that." Interview with Jim Walsh, Jan. 10, 2012.

37—"When Anne, Alice, Joan, Julia and Sue got home…polio germs that might be in the house." Julia Walsh Willkom memoirs, 2006.

37—"It was very quiet in our home…wondering what was going on." Notes from Anne Walsh Colby, September 2006.

38—"For the next several days…wanted to come home." Anne Walsh's letter to her children and grandchildren.

38—"Lorraine stayed at home… Aunt Daisy, who walked down Baker Road to help with the little ones…Full-time bed rest was the order of the day." Julia Walsh Willkom memoirs, 2006.

CHAPTER 5: The Dreaded Disease

39-40—"In truth few doctors knew…Both vaccines cause the body to produce antibodies that fight the polio virus." *March of Dimes.com.*

40-41—"A third virologist actually developed an oral polio vaccine…Dr. Koprowski was a polarizing figure with few advocates in the scientific world." *New York Times*, April 20, 2013.

41—"In addition, Dr. Salk had a huge ally…gave Dr. Salk the edge he needed." *Splendid Solution: Jonas Salk and the Conquest of Polio*, by Jeffrey Kluger.

41—"Within a few years…the world has never been closer to eliminating polio." *The Washington Post*, May 2015, and *USA Today*, Sept. 26, 2015.

CHAPTER 6: Brown Paper Bags #2, #3, #4 and #5

43—"Dave complained…She saw nothing." Anne Walsh's letter to her children and grandchildren in the 1980s.

43-44—"After all the children except Dave…to help our stricken children." Anne Walsh's letter to her children and grandchildren.

44—"That morning when Dave's high school chemistry teacher…'Oh, no,' replied a startled Mr. Slabaugh." Interview with Dan McCullough, May 31, 2012.

44—"Many of the guys…were scared they might get polio, too." Interviews with Mike Dolan, July 5, 2011, and Jack Walsh, Aug. 8, 2011.

44—"Almost immediately the boys stopped playing touch football." Interview with Karen Holland Reddy.

45—"Soon after hearing the latest news…in case one of us might start to feel sick." Julie Walsh Willkom memoirs, 2006.

45—"Aunt Teresa…talked to Mom through the porch window." Lorraine Walsh Vormezeele notes, October 2006.

45-46—"On Saturday, Sept. 10, when Mom and Dad went to visit…I don't think I could stand it if we had to take Dave out of the hospital in the condition Rose was in." Anne Walsh's letter to her children and grandchildren.

46-47—"Father Driscoll acted immediately…Anne, twins Joan and Julie, Sue Frances and Molly." *The Rockford Morning Star*, Sept. 14, 1955.

47—"I was (at school) three days and then I had to quit." *The Beloit Daily News*, Sept. 14, 1955.

47—"Despite the quarantine…feeding the animals and milking the cows." Anne Walsh Colby notes, September 2006.

47—"Lorraine, with help…the college refunded all her money." Lorraine Walsh Vormezeele notes, October 2006, and Anne Walsh Colby notes, September 2006.

47-48—"Monday morning was barely unfolding when a phone call…'would get Dave back on his feet,' Mom said." Anne Walsh's letter to her children and grandchildren.

48—"Dave was in an oxygen tent…permanent brain damage." *United Press,* Sept. 14, 1955.

48—"'We have to keep quiet…a neighbor just sent over a tiddlywinks set.'" *The Beloit Daily News,* Sept. 14, 1955.

48-49—"Speaking to a Chicago Herald-American reporter…it's as though we were picked out." *The Chicago Herald-American*, Sept. 14, 1955.

49—"The county Public Health Department…never could identify a source for the disease." Julie Walsh Willkom memoirs, 2006.

49—"Meanwhile, Dr. Leonard was working…too long to become effective." *The Rockford Morning Star*, Sept. 20, 1955.

49-50—"At least Bernie had been vaccinated…got back on the bus and went back to Durand." Bernie Walsh notes, January 2008.

50—"The day was still young when Dr. Leonard decided Julie…then developed symptoms again." *The Beloit Daily News*, Sept. 14, 1955.

50—"I remember how dark and cold…I had polio." Julie Walsh Willkom memoirs, 2006.

51—"Once again Mom and Dad…help him and all of us best by attending the service." Mom's letter to her children and grandchildren and Julie Walsh Willkom memoirs, 2006.

51—"Earlier that day…special prayer meeting for him." *The Rockford Morning Star*, Sept. 14, 1955.

51-52—"Midway through the St. Mary's service…'had come to offer words of comfort and hope and newspaper men,' Mom said." Anne Walsh's letter to her children and grandchildren.

52—"The news media had become 'the biggest problem…were bound to get it one way or the other.'" Interview with Ken Krienke, Oct. 17, 2006.

52—"Julie's first full day at Township…made her nauseated and gave her headaches." Julie Walsh Willkom memoirs, 2006.

53—"The next day, on Thursday, Sept. 15, Joan's symptoms worsened…containing Joan's clothes." Anne Walsh's letter to her children and grandchildren.

53—"She developed a rigid back…she would do anything to be with her twin." *The Rockford Morning Star*, Sept. 17, 1955.

53—"The hard-working, deeply religious farm couple…I'm sure everything will come out all right.'" *The Rockford Morning Star*, Sept. 18, 1955.

53-54—"The offers of support, financial and moral…'we need all the prayers we can get.'" *The Beloit Daily News*, Sept. 14, 1955.

CHAPTER 7: "Strike It Rich"

57—"One evening during this hectic week…CBS-TV game show 'Strike It Rich.'" *The Rockford Morning Star,* Sept. 16, 1955, and Anne Walsh's letter to her children and grandchildren in the 1980s.

57-58—"At first Dad declined the offer…the flight from Chicago to New York and back." *The Rockford Morning Star*, Sept. 16 and 17, 1955.

58—"Lorraine was a reluctant…was scared to death." Lorraine Walsh Vormezeele notes, October 2006.

58—"She packed her charcoal wool suit…borrowed Marge McCorkle's shoes for Lorraine to wear." Anne Walsh Colby notes, September 2006, and Mary Lou Walsh notes, 2002.

58—"She managed to smile for photographers…Aunt Margaret told the reporters." *The Rockford Morning Star*, Sept. 16, 1955.

58—"At the same time, Dr. Leonard declared…as she enters advance stages of spinal polio." *The Beloit Daily News*, Sept. 16. 1955.

58—"The departure at 3:45 p.m.…the National Foundation of Infantile Paralysis." *The Rockford Morning Star*, Sept. 16, 1955.

58—"Upon landing at Midway Airport…reporters wanting to ask her questions." Lorraine Walsh Vormezelle notes, October 2006.

59—"…Prince George Hotel, on East 28th Street…home for homeless and low-income people." Wikopedia.com.

59—"Lorraine's first task…like the ones that go over our place. Love, Lorraine." Lorraine Walsh Vormezeele notes, October 2006, and actual post card.

59—"Later in the day…'I got an iced tea,' Aunt Margaret said." Notes from Margaret Walsh.

59-60—"The next morning, another escort arrived...'you couldn't get as much as a loaf of bread.'" *The Rockford Morning Star*, Sept. 17, 1955.

60—"Time out also was taken...who were studying for the priesthood." Father Jerry Walsh notes, Sept. 16, 2006.

60—"Julie watched the television show...Ed was sleeping." *The Rockford Register-Republic*, Sept. 16, 1955.

60-61—"After the show ended...'by people who were just passing by.'" *The Rockford Morning Star*, Sept. 17, 1955, and Margaret Walsh notes.

61-62—"Office space at the bank was limited...Virginia and Ruth Flynn, from St. Patrick's Catholic Church in Irish Grove." Notes from Bill Smith.

CHAPTER 8: Cards, Letters and Visitors

63—"As Dave's and Ed's condition continued to slowly improve...'a great deal of anxiety about our children,' Dad said." *The Rockford Morning Star*, Sept. 18, 1955.

63—"Some of that anxiety...'several times a day for several day,' Mom said." Notes from Frances Walsh McGinnis, February 2005, and Anne Walsh's letter to her children and grandchildren.

63-64—"Nevertheless, Dad granted a reporter...'And the Methodists held prayer meetings, too.'" *The Chicago Herald-American*, Sept. 18, 1955.

64—"Back at the parish house...'That's the kind of family it is.'" *The Rockford Morning Star*, Sept. 18, 1955.

64—"At St. Anthony's, Rose was sitting up...letters to them from friends, relatives and strangers." *The Rockford Register-Republic*, Sept. 17, 1955.

64—"*The Rockford Morning Star* published...letters from lots of potential suitors." Julie Walsh Willkom memoirs, 2006.

64—"There were so many that mailman...nearly every day for weeks." Lorraine Walsh Vormezeele notes, October 2006.

68—"One evening while we were on our knees...we finished praying." Julie Walsh Willkom memoirs, 2006.

70—"Dave's classmates Jack Walsh, Bob Haggerty....to pray that he wouldn't get sick." Jack Walsh interview, Aug. 8, 2011.

70—"For many visitors, seeing Dave and Ed...'They remained part of our group wherever they were.'" Interviews with Karen Holland Reddy, Jan. 23, 2012, Harry Vale, Nov. 16, 2011, Al McCartney, May 16, 2012, and Bill Flynn, May 15, 2012, and notes from Bev Meier Waller, 2002.

70-71—"Joan and Julie's visitors...The reporter had contacted the actress." Julie Walsh Willkom memoirs, 2006.

71—"On Monday, Sept. 19, the 'Strike It Rich'...a note typed on business stationery." *The Rockford Morning Star*, Sept. 24, 1955.

71-72—"That week was a special one...you can hear him all the way to Durand." *The Rockford Register-Republic*, Sept. 21, 1955.

CHAPTER 9: Off to Chicago

75—"Joan and Julie's room…Rose 'was always a happy little girl.'" Julie Walsh Willkom memoirs, 2006.

76-77—"Dr. Leonard announced that Dave would be transferred…Parties planned by classmates greeted all of them." *The Rockford Morning Star*, Oct. 7, 1955.

77—"Meanwhile, the fund for our family…staying in the iron lung only at night." *The Rockford Morning Star*, Oct. 9, 1955.

78—"One morning, several of them arrived at our farm…15 women from St. Anne's Sodality of St. Mary's Church served dinner." *The Rockford Morning Star*, Oct. 21, 1955, Bill Walsh notes, October 2006, and interview with Jim Walsh, Jan. 10, 2012 (Jim provided Uncle Laurence Dolan's comment about wagons looking like the grapes of wrath).

79—Aunt Mary visited Dave…she thinks you will do well in Chicago." Letter dated Oct. 22, 1955, from Mary Mulcahy to Dave Walsh.

79-81—"His departure from Rockford Township Hospital…the month ended with the fund for our family reaching $8,000." *The Rockford Morning Star*, Oct. 28, 1955.

CHAPTER 10: Much to Be Thankful For

85-86—"One night Dad and I were in charge…our prayers were answered." Lorraine Walsh Vormezeele notes, October 2006, and Julie Walsh Willkom memoirs, 2006.

86—"Molly remembers…she had frequent checkups for the next few months." Molly Walsh Johnson interview, Sept. 29, 2015.

86—"Today the pupil…her vision is OK." Julie Walsh Willkom memoirs, 2006.

86-87—"Meanwhile, Dave continue to make progress…Rose… was fitted with a corset to support her weakened abdominal muscles." *The Rockford Morning Star*, Nov. 5, 1955.

87—"Barely a day passed when Dave…all of us took turns going with her." Julia Walsh Willkom memoirs, 2006.

87—"Once, Bill joined Mom…didn't get home until 2 o'clock in the morning." Bill Walsh notes, October 2006.

87—"Dr. Janet Wolter, the assistant director…when Mom used her apartment." Interview with Dr. Wolter Aug. 20, 2012.

87—"Nine members of the newly formed high school Letterman's Club…they all went to Research Hospital to visit Dave." *The Durand Gazette*, Nov. 10, 1955.

87-88—"Bob Haggerty planned the many trips…But they went anyway." Jack Walsh interview, Aug. 8, 2011.

88—"On one visit, Dave asked them…Dave sipped it through a straw." Interview with Mike Dolan, July 5, 2011.

88—"Back in Rockford at St. Anthony's…had to be put back into the iron lung." *The North West News*, Nov. 17, 1955.

88—"In Durand a week later…Norm Chilton led Durand with 22 points." *The Durand Gazette*, Nov. 19, 1955.

88—"Tom Dolan and Dave McCullough pretended…played them for Dave." Interview with Tom Dolan, May 7, 2015, and Oct. 27, 2015.

88-89—"On Thanksgiving Eve, Nov. 23, our family celebrated…which Durand won 45-42." *The Durand Gazette*, Nov. 24, 1955.

89—"'God must sure be taking good care of us'…the fund to help our family had now reached $9,302.41." *The Rockford Morning Star*, Nov. 24, 1955.

89-90—"Mom wrote a postcard…'Mr. and Mrs. Keron Walsh." The actual postcard, November 1955.

90-91—"At this Thanksgiving time we want to publicly thank you…Keron and Anne Walsh and family." *The Durand Gazette*, Nov. 24, 1955.

CHAPTER 11: A Reunion for Dave and Ed

93-94—"Pictures of Black Angus cattle and Hampshire hogs…'That's one of the best things,' he said." *The Chicago Herald-American*, Dec. 7, 1955.

94—"Another letter, this one from Belgium…'remember us in their prayers.'" *The Rockford Morning Star*, Dec. 23, 1955.

94-95—"A Christmas newsletter…'but I don't think we should forget David.'" *FFA Newsletter*, February 1956.

95—"As Christmas neared…'we'll still open our gifts on Christmas Eve the way we always do.'" *The Rockford Morning Star*, Dec. 23, 1955.

95—"Christmas morning was busy…so that Dad would have more time with our family." Anne Walsh's letter to her children and grandchildren.

95-96—"Dad and our twin sisters Alice and Anne attended a Christmas party… 'David looks much better in person than he does in newspaper pictures,' Dr. Leonard said." *The Rockford Register-Republic*, Dec. 27, 1955.

96—"Moving Day—Wednesday, Dec. 28…Dad, Mom, Anne and Julie followed in their own car." *The Rockford Register-Republic*, Dec. 28, 1955.

96-97—"As soon as they arrived at the hospital…'but sometimes it takes patients a little while to make the switch." *The Rockford Morning Star*, Dec. 29, 1955.

CHAPTER 12: A New Crisis

99—"Chicago's WLS radio station…updates on Dave and Ed's condition." Aunt Pat Kenucane notes.

99—"On Jan. 4, Julie was listening…Ed's body had taken on a greenish tint." Julie Walsh Willkom memoirs, 2006.

99-100—"Worse yet, Ed fell into a coma…'he's crying all over the place' because of his brother's ordeal." *The Rockford Morning Star*, Jan. 6 and 7, 1956.

100—"By Monday, Jan. 9, Ed's condition…were joined over the weekend by Aunt Theresa Houghton." *The Rockford Morning Star*, Jan. 10, 1956.

101—"On Wednesday, Jan. 11, Ed's lung filled…he was still in a semi=conscious state." *The Rockford Morning Star,* Jan. 12, 1956.

101—"Mom's vigil at Ed's bedside…'dreaded disease until it's wiped out.'" *The Rockford Morning Star*, Jan. 22, 1956.

101—"Ed's condition stabilized but remained…'this is a long process.'" *The Rockford Morning Star,* Feb. 16, 1956.

101—"The official also said Ed's body…never could discover the underlying cause." *The Rockford Morning Star*, Feb. 13, 1956.

101-102—"Alice recalls Mom using the term…often wondered afterward if it was the right decision." Alice Walsh Kraiss notes, 2004-2011.

102—"During Ed's ordeal…he was 'in very good spirits.'" *The Rockford Morning Star,* Feb. 16, 1956.

102—"Dave's first letter…'second day on the typewriter?'" Letter written by Dave to Mom dated Jan. 26, 1956.

102—"Except for a few days…Dad, Aunt Teresa, Aunt Margaret, Aunt Nita and some of our sisters." *The Durand Gazette*, Feb. 4 and 18, 1956.

102—"…Once she left the hospital briefly…It was the first time she noticed her hair had turned white." Mary Lou Walsh notes, 2002.

CHAPTER 13: A Special Graduation

103—"The party at Illinois Research Hospital…Jane Walsh, Joyce Wise and Ken Waller." *The Rockford Morning Star,* March 4, 1956, and *The Beloit Daily News*, March 5, 1956. The Daily News article was written by Mrs. Ward Waller, Mike Waller's mother.

103-104—"An exception was Roger Sarver…It was almost too much to watch, Roger said." Interview with Roger Sarver, July 10, 2011.

104—"Another school friend, Carole Cowan…his condition and voice were much weaker than Dave's." Interview with Carole Cowan Dolan.

104—"Another occasional visitor was Sandy Berg…All I can say is that they brightened my day." Sandy Berg interview, June 1, 2011.

104—"Another regular visitor in Chicago was a priest…remained so for the next several years." Alice Walsh Kraiss notes, 2004-2011.

104-105—"Our sister Anne remembers seeing…even some with expectant mothers." Anne Walsh Colby notes, October 2006.

105—"For months she wrote Dave nearly every day…Anne nearly always signed her letters, 'Love and Prayers.'" Anne Walsh Colby letters, October 1955—June 1956.

105-106—"In early April, all of our hopes were raised…attendants were considering removing them." *The Rockford Morning Star*, April 8, 1956.

106-107—"The doctor called Mom into his office and shocked her with his news...began building a room where the boys would stay." Mom's letter to her children and grandchildren.

107—"Back on the farm, where spring...all I want to do is plow and ride my pony." *The Rockford Morning Star*, May 6, 1956.

107—"Lorraine also helped in the fields...preparing the fields for planting oats." *The Rockford Morning Star*, May 6, 1956.

107—"Dave and Ed continued to be tutored...special agricultural classes." *The Rockford Morning Star*, June 3, 1956.

107-109—"On May 29, Dave's classmates received their diplomas...'It sure feels great to have this diploma,' he said." *The Rockford Morning Star* and *The Rockford Register-Republic,* June 4, 1956, and *The Chicago Tribu*ne, June 4, 1956.

CHAPTER 14: Celebrating Durand's Centennial

111—"To celebrate completion of the barn...this time featuring the Bill Hartwig Band from Wisconsin." *The Durand Gazette,* October 1956.

111—'...it was composed of several area men, including Bill Flynn and Jon Dixon..." Bill Flynn interview on May 15, 2012.

112—"Plans called for it to be large enough...operating in case of power failure." Julie Walsh Willkom memoirs, 2006.

112—"During the construction, Bill, Bernie and Tom...'tear up a piece of the floor to try to retrieve it,' Bernie said." Bernie Walsh notes, January 2008.

112—"It was gone forever, my 'blanky'...Rose made Fran a new red blanket." Fran Walsh McGinnis notes, Feb. 2005.

112—"...it looked absolutely beautiful with knotty pine walls...for around-the-clock nursing care." Julie Walsh Willkom memoirs, 2006.

113—"...Several classmates visited him in early July...Mom was with Ed on his actual birthdate, July 13." *The Durand Gazette*, July 6, 1956, and *The Rockford Morning Star,* July 14, 1956.

113-114—"Ward Waller...had been in the job only three months...who was electrocuted in a farmhouse accident in Shirland." *Durand's Marvelous Merchants,* 2007.

114—"To the fanfare of music by Dulse Liston's 10-piece band...June Raddatz, Sandra Bliss, Betty Keller, Pat Smith, Sandra Tallakson and Delores Davis." *The Durand Gazette*, July 19, 1956.

114-115—"The next afternoon, in the Centennial's official opening ceremony... attorney John B. Anderson and Durand Mayor Ernest Baker." *The Rockford Morning Star,* July 13, 1956.

115—"That evening at the opening of the pageant...the pageant drew more than 5,500 in four nights." *The Durand Gazette,* July 19, 1956.

115—"Years later, Lorraine said she was certain...We had an interesting tour of the city." Lorraine Walsh Vormezeele notes, October 2006.

115—"On Saturday, July 14, in Chicago…a suction device attached to his mouth to help him swallow." *The Rockford Morning Star*, July 15, 1956.

115—"A huge crowd of more than 15,000,…to pass the reviewing stand." *The Durand Gazette*, July 19, 1956.

115-116—"'Dave was to be in Aunt Margaret and Uncle Leonard's…placed him on the rocking bed.'" Lorraine Walsh Vormezeele notes, October 2006.

116---"When Julie saw Dave for the first time…until he asked for someone to move them now and then." Julie Walsh Willkom memoirs, 2006.

116-117—"Meanwhile, banker Art Johnson…the polio chapter took over expenses on June 1." *The Rockford Morning Star,* July 14, 1956.

CHAPTER 15: Broken Hearts

125—"Two weeks after the Centennial…'the new garage we are building.'" Letter dated Aug. 2, 1956, from Paul G. Norsworthy to Dave.

125—"…poor little Eddie started…looking like purple grapes in his lung." Anne Walsh Colby notes, October 2006.

125—"Julie was downstairs at home…She hung up and told us the horrible news." Julie Walsh Willkom memoirs, 2006.

126—"I had never felt so sad…" Julie Walsh Willkom memoirs, 2006.

126—"…died early in the morning of Aug. 21 after having an emergency tracheotomy." *The Rockford Register-Republic*, Aug. 21, 1956.

126—"'…not even raise a finger to wipe away his own tears,' Mom said." Anne Walsh's letter to her children and grandchildren.

126—"So now instead of arranging…body brought home for the wake." Julie Walsh Willkom memoirs, 2006.

126—"…he had visited Dave and Ed in Chicago…I didn't want to spend more time with Ed that day…" Bernie Walsh notes, January 2008.

127—"The death certificate…due to poliomyelitis (late effect)." The actual death certificate filed Aug. 21, 1956.

127—"The planning and work for the wake…waxing all the tile floors." Julie Walsh Willkom memoirs, 2006.

127—"'Everyone seemed to have a bucket…house need to be cleaned.'" Sue Walsh Cocoma notes.

127-128—"'We cleaned through our tears'…rosary and other prayers for Ed.'" Julie Walsh Willkom memoirs, 2006.

128—"The house was especially quiet…to comfort Mom and Dad and all of us.'" Lorraine Walsh Vormezeele notes, October 2006, and Julie Walsh Willkom memoirs, 2006.

128—"Bill served as the Doorman…the line would never end." Bill Walsh notes,

October 2006.

128—"In the early evening, Father Driscoll...began its slow journey to Durand and St. Mary's." Julie Walsh Willkom memoirs, 2006.

128—"The church bells tolled...'It was very touching and sad...'" Interview with Betty Felder, Dec. 8, 2013.

128—"Tom and Mike Dolan...Dave and Dan McCullough served as pall bearers." Interviews with Tom Dolan, April 26, 2012, and Dan McCullough, May 31, 2012.

128—"Bev Waller said that she...on the west side of the aisle." Bev Meier Waller interview.

129-129—"I don't remember many details...everyone laughed, except some of our aunts, who wondered if the comment was appropriate to be said to a priest." Anne Walsh Colby notes, October 2006, and Julie Walsh Willkom memoirs, 2006.

CHAPTER 16: Home at Last

131 —"...officials at Illinois Research Hospital immediately began planning... 'they don't want to disappoint him by putting him in another hospital.'" *The Rockford Morning Star,* Sept. 1, 1956.

131-132—"Mrs. Carrie Fowler of Brodhead, Wis...'it indicates he's doing plenty of the work himself.'" *The Rockford Morning Star*, Sept. 8, 1956.

132-133—"...Doctors placed Dave in the back...the thought of having his oldest son home." *The Rockford Morning Star,* Sept. 9, 1956.

133—"When Dave got home...so someone could place his hand on the grass." Alice Walsh Kraiss notes, 2004-2011.

133—"Waiting at the farm...once he was settled in and comfortable." *The Rockford Morning Star*, Sept. 9, 1956.

133—"And we were delighted to have him home...'we had to act quickly before the head of the bed started down again.'" Julie Walsh Willkom memoirs, 2006.

133—"'Dave ate well...After helping them I decided to be a nurse." Alice Walsh Kraiss notes, 2004-2011.

134—"One of the earliest visitors was Al McCartney...'I can sit in a wheelchair and do the books." Al McCartney interview, May 16, 2012.

135—"We would shut the glass doors...instead of the other way around." Julie Walsh Willkom memoirs, 2006.

135—"One of the most faithful visitors was Norm Chilton...Norm had just met our Grandpa and Grandma Kenucane." Norm Chilton interview, April 20, 2013.

135—"When Aunt Pat brought...'because it makes Grandma dizzy." Pat Kenucane notes.

135—"Cousin Tom Dolan...the previous season's Durand High School basketball games." Tom Dolan interview, November 2015.

135-136—"The team wasn't very good...third in the Stephenson County Confer-

ence with a 4-6 record." Durand High School Yearbook of 1956.

136—"Father Driscoll was a frequent visitor…was given a sturdy chair and ate his scrambled eggs." Sue Walsh Cocoma notes.

136-137—"Giving Dave a bath…Dave was slowly lowered into the water." Sue Walsh Cocoma notes and notes of other sisters.

137—"Dave enjoyed being around most of his nurses…the lawsuit was dismissed." Julie Walsh Willkom memoirs, 2006.

137—"…One night the nurse fell asleep…'so I got up to check,' he said." Alice Walsh Kraiss notes, 2004-2011.

138—"'Rose started school this year,' Mom said…the brace extended from the pelvis to the chin and the back of the head." *The Rockford Register-Republic*, Jan 19, 1957.

138—"About the same time, on March 4…lots of visits from friends and relatives." *The Durand Gazette*, March 1957.

138—"Seven weeks later, on April 22…Later, she had another five vertebrae operated on." *The Rockford Morning Star*, April 23, 1957.

138-139—"The Class of 1957 also dedicated…'His courage will always be admired by us.'" Durand High School Yearbook of 1957.

139—"In addition, the Student Council…a plaque in memory of Ed…" *The Durand Gazette*, May 1957.

139—"…One of the most touching visits…it was a special treat for Dave and all of us." Sue Walsh Cocoma notes.

139—"Five days later, Dave's stay at home ended…taking over the duty from the McHenry line to the hospital in Chicago." *The Rockford Morning Star*, June 21, 1957.

CHAPTER 17: More Broken Hearts

143—"Dave was back in the hospital less than three weeks when Rose…So was Aunt Margaret." Julie Walsh Willkom memoirs, 2006, and Anne Walsh Colby notes, October 2006.

143—"…But the surgery never occurred…plunging him into critical condition for several weeks." *The Rockford Morning Star*, Sept. 4, 1957.

143—"Dave, the fun-loving boy…Mom was at his side." *The Rockford Morning Star*, Sept. 4, 1957.

143—"…but the death certificate listed it as 11:30 a.m.…'and bilateral renal calculi…'" The death certificate filed Sept. 4, 1957.

143-144—"Several of Mom's sisters…She went to bed exhausted and absolutely grief stricken." Julie Walsh Willkom memoirs, 2006.

144—"The next night many of us…'had loads of fun in our big group.'" Anne Walsh Colby notes, October 2006.

144—"…the planning and work for Dave's wake…it was surrounded by flowers

and large candles." Julie Walsh Willkom memoirs, 2006.

144—**"Bill again served as the Doorman…on both sides of Baker Road."** Bill Walsh notes, October 2006.

144—**"Bernie recalled seeing Dad cry and 'wishing he didn't have to do that.'"** Bernie Walsh notes, January 2008.

144—**"The parade of cars seemed endless…'I thought my heart would break,' Anne said."** Anne Walsh Colby notes, October 2006.

144-145—**"As Mom entered the church vestibule…didn't want to talk to reporters anymore."** Bernie Walsh notes, January 2008.

145—**"Dr. Janet Wolter, who helped…she did have a chance to speak with Mom and Dad."** Dr. Janet Wolter Grip notes, Dec. 8, 2015.

145—**"During the Mass, our cousin Jerry…saw the reflection of the Virgin Mary ceiling mural on top of Dave's casket."** Alice Walsh Kraiss notes, 2004-2011.

145—**"Jack Walsh thinks he was one, but wasn't sure."** Jack Walsh interview, December 2015.

145—**"Only one person…two of the pall bearers were Tom Spelman and Dave's classmate Bill Rogers."** Jim Walsh interview, Jan. 10, 2012.

CHAPTER 18: Tom Dolan's Poem

149-151—All of the information in this chapter came from a letter from Tom Dolan to Rose Walsh Landers in April 2015 and in several interviews with Tom Dolan, the last being in November 2015.

CHAPTER 19: How Did We Defeat Polio?

153-154—**"Once, on a cold winter day, Dad came…They are the same. They are not good."** Julie Walsh Willkom memoirs, 2006.

154—**"Another time Dad, in a moment of grief…he quickly realized he had three other outstanding sons."** Lorraine Walsh Vormezeele notes, October 2006.

154—**"When Molly was taken to the hospital…She implored Him to take her."** Chris Cocoma interview.

154—**"Mom and Dad were able to cope…because of their faith."** Lorraine Walsh Vormezeele notes October 2006.

154—**"The prayers that were sent up…are probably what kept us all sane."** Anne Walsh Colby notes October 2006.

154—**"How we prayed the rosary…What an example!"** Alice Walsh Kraiss notes, 2004-2011.

154-155—**"Mom and Dad certainly earned…wonderful job of passing it on to their children."** Joan Walsh Didier notes, 2015.

155—**"Where could Mother and Dad…they continued fervent, quiet prayer."** Julie Walsh Willkom memoirs, 2006.

155—"Her deep faith sustained your Mom...he carried on courageously." Aunt Margaret Walsh letter to Rose.

155—"I think our families were welded together...there is an inner strength that we all could use if we just had her faith." Mary Lou Walsh notes, 2002.

155-156—"We did what we had to do...I would sometimes think about this book and its message, and it helped me." Anne Walsh's comments to her son-in-law, Bill Landers, 1987.

CHAPTER 20: Life Resumes

158—"Lorraine and Bob Vormezeele were engaged...they returned to our house to change their clothes and then left for their honeymoon..." Lorraine Walsh Vormezeele notes, 2006.

158—"Alice enrolled in St. Anthony's School of Nursing...while helping Dave when he was at home." Alice Walsh Kraiss notes, 2004-2011.

158—"Anne...was accepted at the Congregation...changed her mind about the convent." Anne Walsh Colby notes, 2006.

159—"Autumn was a melancholy time for Mom...Dad told her it was a harvest moon." Alice Walsh Kraiss notes, 2004-2011.

159—"...Bill, as the sixth man, was one of the most valuable players on the team that compiled the school's best record of 25-2." Coach Sid Felder interview, 2006.

159—"...he showed the Grand Champions steer...the purchase of $1,278 was made by the First National Bank and Trust Co. in Rockford." *The Rockford Morning Star,* August 1963.

160—"One of her teachers was Cres Vale...'she was a delight to work with." Cres Vale interview, Nov. 16, 2011.

161—"We selected a huge fallen white oak tree...to celebrate a special Mass and dedicate the white oak sculpture." *The Volunteer,* July 22, 1993, and *Chip Chats Magazine,* May-June 1994.

CHAPTER 21: Whatever Happened to All of Us?

Information for all the mini-biographies of people and institutions in this chapter came from Walsh family members and records, Dr. Janet Wolter Grip, Jack Walsh, Norm Chilton, Dan McCullough, Beverly Meier Waller, Roger Sarver, Harry and Cres Vale, St. Anthony's Medical Center's website, Wikopedia.com and obituaries over the years in *The Durand Gazette, The Volunteer* and *The Rockford Morning Star.*

Photos and pictures of headlines and articles from The Rockford Morning Star *and the* Rockford Register-Republic *were used with permission from* The Rockford Register Star *and rrstar.com.*

ACKNOWLEDGEMENTS

We must first recognize and thank our brothers and sisters for their extensive notes and memoirs written over several years recording their memories of our family's polio ordeal. They are: Lorraine Walsh Vormezeele, Anne Walsh Colby, Alice Walsh Kraiss, Joan Walsh Didier, Julie Walsh Willkom, Bill Walsh, Bernie Walsh, Tom Walsh, Fran Walsh McGinnis and Molly Walsh Johnson. Their contributions were enormous and priceless. We also owe Julie an extra dose of gratitude for compiling the facts for the Walsh biographies and offering dozens of helpful suggestions, especially as our adviser for medical terms.

We also must thank all of our relatives who often wrote detailed notes and/or allowed us to interview them about their recollections of those years. They include Aunt Margaret Walsh, Aunt Pat Kenucane, Aunt Teresa Houghton, Mary Lou Walsh, Father Jerry Walsh, Jim Walsh, Florence Walsh, Bob Vormezeele, Christopher Cocoma, Sister Mary Dolan, Tom Dolan, Mike Dolan, Charlotte Dolan Borgogni, Jack Walsh and Bill Haggerty.

Our gratitude also goes to many friends who gave us their time and energy by granting us interviews and writing us notes of recollection. They include Norm Chilton, Ken Krienke, Dan McCullough, Beverly Meier Waller, Sally Stetler Waller, David and Frances Waller, Carole Cowan Dolan, Roger Sarver, Bill Flynn, Judy Johnson, Karen Holland Reddy, Beverly Fosler Lewis, Dorothy Schwartz, Mary Robinson, Sandy Berg, Betty Felder, Dr. Janet Wolters Grip, Harry and Cres Vale, Bill Steward, Bill Smith, Al McCartney and Msgr. Thomas C. Brady.

We are grateful to other friends — Mary McMurrer, Sue

Schnieders and Rick and Donna Williams — for encouraging Rose to write her family's polio story and who helped in many other ways to complete the project. Many thanks also go to the staff of The Printing House in Iowa City

We also are in debt to Sherry McKenna Meinert, who writes the "Not So Long Ago…" column in the weekly Durand newspaper, *The Volunteer*. Whenever we needed a newspaper clip or another piece of information, Sherry always could find it.

We especially want to thank our designer and producer, Jean D. Dodd, for creating such an outstanding design.

A special thanks of appreciation goes to Sue's husband, John Cocoma, and her children for supporting her while working to help Rose complete her dream.

Finally, we are grateful beyond words to Bill Landers, Rose's loving husband who over the last three decades has supported Rose's goal of writing a book about our family's polio crisis. Bill's moral support, and that of their three children, has been constant for 10 years. During the past year, Bill has been Rose's faithful project assistant "extraordinaire." Our authors' team would not have been able to function without Bill's help.

Rose Walsh Landers and Sue Walsh Cocoma
April 1, 2016

ABOUT THE AUTHORS

Rose Walsh Landers

Rose Landers graduated from Durand High School in 1968 and earned her B.A. degree in history, with an emphasis in journalism from Western Illinois University in Macomb in 1972. She planned to pursue a career in journalism but switched gears to health care during her senior year at WIU. In December 1974, Rose completed the Occupational Therapy (OT) certificate program at the University of Pennsylvania in Philadelphia. In February 1975, she moved to Iowa for her first OT job at the University of Iowa's Hospital School. It was the beginning of her 30-year career as a part-time pediatric occupational therapist, which included 20 years in the public schools. In 1977 she married Bill Landers, a special education teacher at Hospital School. They raised their three children,  Bridget, Matthew and Michael, in Iowa City and now have five young grandchildren. Until age 60, Rose was active and independent, enjoying road trips to visit her children and other family members. She savored her leisurely evening bike rides, and still misses them. In 2013, she was diagnosed with Primary Lateral Sclerosis (PLS), a slow form of ALS, or Lou Gehrig's disease. The effects are complicated by the polio residuals. She now relies on a wheelchair and uses an iPad to communicate.

— rwalsland@gmail.com

Sue Walsh Cocoma

Sue Cocoma graduated from Durand High School in 1961 and in 1965 from the college her big sister Lorraine could not attend. With her teaching degree from Edgewood College in Madison, Sue taught

lower elementary school for 34 years, with an emphasis on kindergarten and second grade. She and her husband John, an engineer for Ingersoll Milling in Rockford for 34 years, raised their five children in Durand. Their four daughters Anne, Katie, Julie and Sarah, and son Christopher all graduated from the same school where their mom taught — Durand Unit 322. Sue remained active in her community and parish during her career and still serves today on the Durand Ecumenical Council. She was honored as the Woman of the Year from St. Mary's and Irish Grove parishes in 2012. John and Sue recently celebrated their 50th wedding anniversary with their five children and nine grandchildren.

suecocoma@hotmail.com

Mike Waller

Mike Waller graduated from Durand High School in 1959 with Joan and Julie Walsh. He joined the staff of *The Decatur Herald* as a sports clerk in 1961 and graduated in 1963 from Millikin University in Decatur, Ill. with a bachelor's degree in history and political science. He worked for the next 15 years as a reporter and editor at the *Herald*,

The Cleveland Plain Dealer, The Courier-Journal and *The Louisville Times*. In 1978 he joined the staff of *The Kansas City Star* and became the only editor in the *Star*'s history to serve in the top three newsroom positions: managing editor of the *Star*, managing editor of *The Kansas City Times* and editor of *The Kansas City Star and Times*.

Waller was named executive editor of *The Hartford Courant* in 1986, became editor of the *Courant* in 1990 and was appointed publisher and CEO in 1994. Three years later he was named publisher and CEO of *The Sun* in Baltimore and senior vice president of The Times Mirror Co. During his 41-year career he worked for newspapers that won dozens of national journalism awards, including eight Pulitzer Prizes. In Hartford and Baltimore, he served on more than 20 boards of civic organizations and was chairman of United Way campaigns

in both cities that raised a total of more than $70 million. He retired at the end of 2002 and he and his wife Donna now live on Hilton Head Island, S.C. Between them, they have four children and three grandchildren. Waller has written two other books: *Durand Marvelous Merchants: A Tale of Small-Town Life and Big-Time Softball* and *Blood on the Out-Basket: Lessons in Leadership from a Newspaper Junkie*. Both are available at amazon.com.

mikeewaller@aol.com

Made in the USA
San Bernardino, CA
29 July 2016